With *A Call to Extraordinary Prayer*, Steve Nation takes us deeply into the book of Acts and reveals how ordinary people can pray extraordinarily. Peppered with historical references to John Calvin, Jonathan Edwards, and many others, this book shows how you and I stand in continuity with countless Christians throughout the ages whose lives orbited around the privilege of prayer. If you want your prayer life informed, reformed, and transformed, read this book.

Christian T. George
Curator of the Spurgeon Library,
Assistant Professor of Historical Theology,
Midwestern Baptist Theological Seminary, Kansas City, Missouri

This book is both a rebuke and an inspiration. It presents an entirely justified corrective to the church (and there are many) which loves solid Bible preaching but happily and regularly neglects the humble prayer meeting. And then we wonder why we do not see people saved. Steve Nation gives many close-to-home examples of how we get it wrong, and many practical suggestions of how to more closely follow the Biblical pattern of church life. The encouragement of the book comes via a descriptive working through of Acts and other New Testament writings to show what a church could and should be by the power of the Holy Spirit. The author is disarmingly honest about our battle with prayerlessness and engagingly practical about how all Christians can have the privilege of participation in this crucial struggle.

Autho ...ton
 ...land

A Call to Extraordinary Prayer is part study of prayer in Acts, and part rally cry to the Church gathered to pray. Read it and you will be greatly encouraged and motivated to pray because we pray to our great God, good and powerful, and the sovereign overseer of our lives. Read it and you will most likely be rebuked as the spotlight is shone on your own prayer life. As Steve reminds the reader: the Church gathered is the Church praying. The challenge is: is that true of us?

Jenny Salt
Dean of students, Sydney Missionary and Bible College, Sydney

Any book that causes me to reflect deeply on whether I am a prayerfully dependent child of God and minister of Christ's Church, and whether our church is truly a strong church, gets a big 'thumbs up' and 'thanks be to God!' *A Call to Extraordinary Prayer* certainly did both those things for me. As a result of reading this book, I've been praying more. As a result of reading this book, I've led the church, and especially the leaders, to be praying more. For this, I and the church God has entrusted me to pastor, thank you.

Ben Ho
Pastor of St Lucia Evangelical Church, Brisbane

This is a book for those who are longing to see a powerful movement of God in the world, their community, their church, and their own heart. it is God-centered rather than man-centered. It is saturated with the Bible rather than techniques. It inspires a sense of awe and excitement about what God might be pleased to do when His people seek Him in earnest prayer.

Mike McKinley
Pastor of Sterling Park Baptist Church, Sterling, Virginia
Author of *Passion*, and *Did the devil make me do it?*

I warmly commend this book for it is biblical, readable and well-illustrated. The author draws attention to important prayer references in Acts in order to 'recall' Christians and churches to 'united prayer'. That is a welcome and much needed emphasis. The reason is that only the Lord can save and also revive His Church in power. The relationship of Word and prayer must be restored in our lives and churches. Please heed this *Call to Extraordinary Prayer*.

Eryl Davies
Heath Church Elder, Cardiff, Wales
Research Supervisor, Union School of Theology, Bridgend/Oxford

This book is clear, warm-hearted and compelling. Steve has done us a real service in presenting this biblical call to prayer to us in a fresh and real way.

Gary Millar
Principal of Queensland Theological College, Brisbane

Steve Nation

A Call to
Extraordinary
Prayer

**Recharging your Prayer Life
through the Book of Acts**

CHRISTIAN
FOCUS

Unless otherwise marked Scripture is taken from the *The Holy Bible, New International Version®*. NIV®, copyright©1973, 1978, 1984 by International Bible Society. Used by permission of Zondervan. All rights reserved.

Scripture quotations marked esv are from *The Holy Bible, English Standard Version*, copyright © 2001 by Crossway Bibles, a publishing ministry of Good News Publishers. Used by permission. All rights reserved. ESV Text Edition: 2011.

Steve Nation is a pastor at St. Matthew's Anglican Church in Wanniassa, Australia.

paperback ISBN 978-1-5271-0089-3
epub ISBN 978-1-5271-0125-8
mobi ISBN 978-1-5271-0126-5

Published in 2017 by
Christian Focus Publications Ltd.,
Geanies House, Fearn, Ross-shire,
IV20 1TW, Great Britain
www.christianfocus.com

Cover design Daniel van Straaten

Printed by Nørhaven, Denmark

Contents

Dedication:
To my wife Keiyeng, and my kids Jakey, Levi and Lucy: my joys and my delight

Acknowledgements

This book would never have seen the light of day without the loving, kind-hearted support of the following people:

+ My wife Keiyeng: who is to me (in all her strength and weakness) as her name declares – 'filled with Christ'.

+ Bruce Winter: who first encouraged me to write then was surprisingly delighted by this book in draft form, and guided me through the process of how, why and where to seek its publishing. What a gift is the friendship and wisdom of an older brother!

+ The prayers of the faithful little church I pastored when it was written (5:17 church). Though 5:17 church no longer gathers, the people who made up this beautiful local body of Christ have been and will continue to be a light and joy to my heart.

+ Willie Mackenzie and the team at Christian Focus – thank you for believing in the message of this book and leading it to publication. May it bless the church as we have hoped it will.

Synopsis

What is a strong church? To be classified as a faithful and Christ-centred church today, a consistent criterion is whether or not the church in focus is a good Bible-teaching church. Of course, this is vital. But what if the church has solid teaching, but is a relatively prayer-less church? Is it still a strong church? The Bible seems to say, unequivocally, no! A strong Biblical church is a church that gives its attention to Word and prayer.

The Book of Acts shows how these two go hand in hand – the link between the ministry of Word and prayer. Acts teaches us that a distinguishing mark of a Christian and of a truly Biblical church is that they pray. The way Christians pray in the Book of Acts is largely corporate in nature. This includes prayer for healing, prayer for sending out missionaries, prayer for church leaders, and prayer for boldness in proclaiming the gospel to an apathetic or hostile world.

This book takes us through Acts, and calls upon God's people to pray for revival in our day – for the gospel to go forth, asking God to bring multitudes of the lost under the Lordship of Christ, and mature His church till we see Him in glory.

Introduction

It's an exciting time to be a Christian. It's an exciting time to be part of the church. If we all stopped and thought for just a moment, the list of people or groups that have been at the forefront of stimulating gospel-growth in individuals, churches, regions and countries would be remarkable. I think we could say with confidence that a significant reformation in doctrine and church practice has occurred – and on quite a large scale. Theology has many gifted teachers, hungry learners, faithful seminaries, thriving and reproducing churches, careful publishing houses, rejuvenated mission agencies, and edifying conference ministries. This is an enormous answer to prayer.

But the question has to be asked: is this enough? Is reformation in doctrine, skills and teaching the sum total of our aims? Most Christians would say very strongly, no! We seek individual and large-scale gospel renewal. But a follow-up question then arises: what are the means that God has given us to grow His church? And are we using those means as biblically prescribed?

The question develops as we ponder: why has this distinct reformation in theology not also translated into large numbers of the non-believing world becoming Christians? Australia, where I live and minister, is seen as hard soil to plant and water the gospel in. The situation is the same in Canada, Europe, and many places in the U.S. So we must stop and think: what is needed to take the solid Bible teaching that many of us know and love, and see the multitudes inside and outside of our churches deeply and eternally changed?

This book will argue that although there has been growth in our theological knowledge and ability to communicate the gospel of grace – that is not enough. It wouldn't even be enough if we mastered theology, biblical interpretation, pastoral skills and methods and missional strategy. Why? Because God has told us in 1 Corinthians 3:5-7 that we can plant (share the gospel) and water (teach the Scriptures), but it's God alone who can bring the growth (regeneration and Christian maturity). This book will argue that only in humble dependence on God will our churches function faithfully. As we plant and water, it is ongoing and dependent prayer that connects with the extraordinary God who can do in and for us what we could never do in our life and ministry.

'An Humble Attempt'

Two hundred and fifty years ago, Jonathan Edwards issued 'An Humble Attempt to promote Explicit Agreement and Visible Union of God's People, in Extraordinary Prayer, for the Revival of Religion and the Advancement of Christ's Kingdom on Earth, Pursuant to Scripture Promises and Prophecies concerning the Last Time'.[1] It's a big title! But it was an even bigger book – not in size, but in purpose and impact. The purpose behind the book was a passionate response to the waning spiritual momentum of the people of Edwards' pastorate after a time of growth. In other words, it was a call for the people of God to bow before their God, in humble dependence, and ask God to awaken

---

1. J. Edwards, *A Call to United, Extraordinary Prayer... An Humble Attempt* (Ross-shire, Scotland; Christian Focus Publications, 2003).

the church to the things of God, so the church of God would recover its first love, and shine as a bright light in the darkness of the world around them.

As Edwards noted in the title of the book – it was a humble attempt. Prayer is humbling. Praying with others is humbling – if it is done with confession, dependence on God, and self-awareness of personal limitations. But why, in our age of technology, solid Bible Colleges and abundant resources, would anyone bother to gather together as God's people, often, and in humble, dependent prayer?

Insufficient

I want to put forward quite a few reasons. But before we get to the Bible, a bit about me. I'm a forty-year-old Caucasian male. I was born in Melbourne, the cosmopolitan capital of Australia. I grew up in Sydney, attending a church yet having little understanding of the glory and grace of Jesus. These years were a mix of the blessing of a strong and stable family whilst struggling through crippling anxiety and depression. It wasn't until I was well into my twenties that I was officially diagnosed with Obsessive Compulsive Disorder (OCD).

Into this mix of joy and pain, confusion and uncertainty, God intervened. I was converted to Christ through the faithful Bible-teaching ministry of a warm and Jesus-loving church. After a few years of learning to grasp and grow in the grace and knowledge of Jesus, I went to Bible College. With the huge number of non-Christians around me I had hopes for a life-long ministry as an evangelist. Then during college my plans were rearranged a little, and I was led into pastoral ministry. For the last ten years, I have been involved in ethnic and multi-cultural churches, mostly in church revitalisation and church planting.

It's been quite a journey. In this time, as I preached most weeks in a small but beautiful congregation, and sought to be faithful in evangelism, I have been convicted of my insufficiency for the task at hand. That church was located in a university suburb, having the (significantly) highest rate of atheists and agnostics in our state. Evangelism is hard. And ministry can be discouraging. But in the midst of this, some Bible verses which are well known, have taken real meaning for life and ministry. They are:

+ Jesus answered him, 'Truly, truly, I say to you, unless one is born again he cannot see the kingdom of God' (John 3:3 ESV).

+ Apart from me you can do nothing (John 15:5).

+ Unless the LORD builds the house, those who build it labour in vain (Ps. 127:1 ESV).

These passages teach us that salvation is a work of God's grace, regenerating the spiritually dead to living faith (John 3, Eph. 2:4-5). It is God who builds His church (Ps. 127:1, Matt. 16:18). It is God who grows His people (1 Cor. 3:6-7). So, here is where Jonathan Edwards' book comes in – a humble attempt at praying for God to:

+ pour out His Spirit to exalt His Son through the gospel

+ save the lost: locally and globally

+ build His church: locally and globally

+ grow His people in the grace and knowledge of Jesus Christ (2 Pet. 3:18)

The motivation for this cannot be because we want to experience a spiritual high. And it cannot be formed out of despising slow growth and the everyday, ordinary experiences of the church. It cannot be because we think we can twist God's arm into doing something bigger or better than what He's doing now. It's because Jesus is seeking and saving the lost (Luke 19:10). He is building His church. He is sovereign, and calls us to pray without ceasing (1 Thess. 5:18).

Revival

Jonathan Edwards' small book was based on Zechariah 8:20-22:

> *This is what the LORD Almighty says: 'Many peoples and the inhabitants of many cities will yet come, and the inhabitants of one city will go to another and say, 'Let us go at once to entreat the LORD and seek the LORD Almighty. I myself am going.' And many peoples and powerful nations will come to Jerusalem to seek the LORD Almighty and to entreat him.*

It was a call to unite in prayer for worldwide revival. And 250 years ago, *An Humble Attempt* was read, heard, heeded, and answered. In God's sovereign grace, it was the precursor to the second and third Great Awakenings – where thousands of individuals were redeemed, and cities and countries transformed. Many since have met together, asking for God to do this again – some using the words of the prophet Habakkuk:

> *O LORD, I have heard the report of you, and your work, O LORD, do I fear. In the midst of the years revive it; in the midst of the years make it known; in wrath remember mercy (Hab. 3:2 ESV).*

Habakkuk's prayer was a call upon God to renew His great work of redemption and renewal in a rebellious, forgetful and idolatrous people. It is a call for revival. J. I. Packer defines revival as: 'A work of God by His Spirit through His Word bringing the spiritually dead to living faith in Christ, and renewing the inner life of Christians who have grown slack and sleepy'.[2]

This definition of revival is helpful – because the awakening we long for is not just for the masses of those outside of Christ, but those in Christ to grow in Christ-likeness. It's not just seeking a large-scale movement, but the transformation of the individual bound down in sinful habits or spiritual lethargy.

Isaiah 55:10-11 has for a long time been a cherished promise that preachers cling to.

> As the rain and the snow come down from heaven, and do not return to it without watering the earth and making it bud and flourish, so that it yields seed for the sower and bread for the eater, so is my word that goes out from my mouth: It will not return to me empty, but will accomplish what I desire and achieve the purpose for which I sent it.

What confidence should we have in the Word of God to do its intended work! Unfortunately, many of us know verses 10-11, but neglect verses 12-13. What will God's Word achieve?

> You will go out in joy and be led forth in peace; the mountains and hills will burst into song before you, and all the trees of the field will clap their hands. Instead of the thornbush will grow the juniper, and instead of briers the myrtle will grow. This will be

---

2. J. I. Packer, *A Quest for Godliness* (Wheaton, Illinois; Crossway, 2010), p. 36.

for the LORD's renown, for an everlasting sign, that will endure
forever.

These verses tell us about an all-of-life (including creation)
renewal. Yes, these verses will be fully realised in the new
heaven and new earth. But as new creations in Christ
(2 Cor. 5:17), there is to be hope and joy and wholehearted
praise and deep spiritual transformation in us. These
words capture some of the wonder and privilege of being
a redeemed child of God. It's the life we want for ourselves
and our church members.

So what do we do? We pray; or at least, we struggle to
pray. We pray with and for our church leaders. We pray
for healing for the sick and struggling. We pray for the lost.
And our churches do prayer meetings; some even organise
concerts of prayer spanning not just churches but cities and
countries. But what is this to look like? And where do we
look for guidance on this?

Reflection Questions

1. Revival for many people in the past 150 years has
    been an evangelistic meeting to invite people to –
    where a similar format of songs, prayer, gospel talk,
    invitation, altar call and follow-up is present. How
    is this picture of revival similar/dissimilar to what
    we've looked at in this chapter?

2. Read the book of Habakkuk. What do you think
    Habakkuk is referring to in 3:2 – in terms of the past
    work of God and what he hoped for, for the future?

1

Why look at prayer in the Book of Acts?

Many find the Book of Acts to be the manual for a wide range of ministries. At its heart, Acts isn't a manual for ministry, but the description of the Acts of the Risen Lord Jesus, His Spirit-empowered disciples and the world-altering Word. It's an exciting read. And what shapes all they did? What empowered all they did? What we will see is that it was consistent, united prayer. In the words of Alan Thompson, 'speeches and prayers introduce, sum up and transition' throughout the Book of Acts. These two features of the early church weave in and out of the narrative:

1. The ministry of the Word:

    *   Those who accepted his message were baptised, and about three thousand were added to their number that day (Acts 2:41).

    *   So the word of God spread (Acts 6:7).

    *   The Lord's hand was with them, and a great number of people believed and turned to the Lord (Acts 11:21).

    *   But the word of God continued to spread and flourish (Acts 12:24).

+ The word of the Lord spread through the whole region (Acts 13:49).

2. The ministry of prayer:

+ They all joined together constantly in prayer (Acts 1:14).

+ They devoted themselves… to prayer (Acts 2:42).

+ One day Peter and John were going up to the temple at the time of prayer (Acts 3:1).

+ When they heard this, they raised their voices together in prayer to God (Acts 4:24).

+ [We] will give our attention to prayer and the ministry of the word (Acts 6:4).

Links connected: the ministry of Word and prayer

The Book of Acts is the paradigm – the link between the ministry of the Word, and the necessity of prayer. Often, people studying Acts focus on the themes of Word ministry, the coming of the Holy Spirit, mission, social concern, signs and wonders etc. But rarely is corporate prayer seen as a key theme in Acts. This is a mistake, not just because of the sheer number of times prayer features in Acts but because of its location in the narrative.[1] And it's not just its location that is important – it is the breadth and depth of prayer that is described in Acts that is truly breathtaking. It is Ephesians 6:18 in action:

---

1. For example, see After Jesus' ascension and the Day of Pentecost (Acts 1:14 and 24); after the Day of Pentecost and the formation of the New Testament church (Acts 2:42); when facing persecution for the first time, post-Pentecost (Acts 4); and in deciding what are to be the priorities of the apostles and elders (Acts 6).

> *And pray in the Spirit on all occasions*
> *With all kinds of prayers and requests.*
> *With this in mind, be alert and always keep on praying*
> *for all the Lord's people.*

Again and again, key moments in redemptive history are preceded by prayer or responded to by prayer – in the Bible, and in the history of the evangelical church. We would do well to heed this call.

We see this in the lead-up to the eighteenth-century spiritual revival that swept through Great Britain and the U.S. The gospel was proclaimed through the ministries of men like George Whitefield, John and Charles Wesley. But preceding this large-scale gospel proclamation, were the dark days following the British Act of Uniformity, where two thousand ministers were ejected from their ministries (and means of living). As Arnold Dallimore summarised:

> Hundreds of these men suffered throughout the rest of their lives, and a number died in prison. Yet these terrible conditions became the occasion of a great volume of prayer; forbidden to preach under threat of severe penalties – as John Bunyan's Bedford imprisonment bore witness – they yet could pray, and only eternity will reveal the relationship between this burden of supplication and the revival that followed.[2]

Why should we be praying for revival? J. I. Packer gave a clear reason when he wrote:

> 'Revival is a social, corporate thing, touching and transforming communities, large and small. Bible prayers for revival implore God to quicken not me but us.... . Revival comes to

---

2. A. Dallimore, *George Whitefield, The Life and Times of the Great Evangelist of the Eighteenth-century Revival: Vol. 1* (Edinburgh; The Banner of Truth Trust, 1979), pp. 19-20.

Christians individually, no doubt, but it is not an isolated, individualistic affair.... God revives His church, and then the new life overflows from the church for the conversion of outsiders and the renovation of society.[3]

It has been noted by some that no passage in Scripture calls upon the church to pray for revival. This is true. But as Martyn Lloyd-Jones points out, 'the church always looks like the church in the New Testament when she is in the midst of revival'. In essence, Lloyd-Jones is saying: you don't pray for God to send revival when you're living in one.[4] The description in Acts of the mass conversion of sinners to Christ and the building up of His church in such dramatic fashion is revival. It is the church doing the usual things of worship, preaching, prayer and evangelism – only with intensified force and results.[5]

For many of us today, we are not in a season of seeing mass conversions to Christ and an alive and flourishing gospel-centred church. This is why we pray – to ask God to send forth His Spirit, and make His Word spread and be honoured amongst the ministries of our church and the missions we support, just as it happened amongst the Thessalonians (1 Thess. 3:1).

Reading Acts as prescriptive or descriptive?

How should we read the Book of Acts? Much ink has been spilled over the issue of the place Acts has in the life of the church today. On one side, Acts should be read as the model on which the present-day church should base

---

3. J. I. Packer, *Keep in Step with the Spirit* (Leicester; IVP, 1984), p. 256.
4. C. Hansen & J. Woodbridge, *A God-Sized Vision*, (Grand Rapids; Zondervan, 2010), p. 26.
5. Hansen & Woodbridge, *A God-Sized Vision*, p. 29.

itself. This is the prescriptive model of reading Acts. In contrast, the descriptive reading of Acts states that the book is simply a narrative of the gospel's progress from Jerusalem to Rome as well as the life of the early church. Which method should we follow? This book takes the view that we should read Acts descriptively, whilst at the same time seeing that the positive picture of Word and prayer ministry should shape our life and ministry today. The New Testament Epistles add to the picture Acts gives us of the New Testament church, as well as prescription on how they and we should function as church.

Reflection Questions

1. Read Acts 1–2. Take a note of every time a Christian or church is praying. What is the context in which these prayers are situated? From these chapters – is the link between prayer and the Word in Acts important?

2. What are the ordinary means God promises to use to convert, redeem and sanctify people?

    +   Are they enough to bring about God's desired purposes?

    +   Why? Why not?

2

Grounded in the gospel, gathered to pray

(Acts 1:13-14; 2:42)

A few years ago, at the church I was at then, we had our annual retreat. It was a time for us to get away into the local mountain air, be challenged with Bible teaching, do silly things in attempts to build community life, and eat copious amounts of junk food. It was a brilliant time! One of the features of that year's retreat was the celebration of three new church members. In the past, whenever someone has 'signed up' as an official member, they've received an official certificate – which they receive with a smile, and probably take it home and carefully file away (most likely to never see the light of day again!). But that year, we decided to do something a little different. We handed out glue sticks to our new members. That's right – glue sticks. This may sound a little strange to some, but the reason can be found in Acts 2:42:

> They devoted themselves to the apostles' teaching and to fellowship, to the breaking of bread and to prayer.

The context is: Pentecost has just happened with the resultant ingathering of 3,000 new believers. Then the first church meeting is described. What we read of in Acts 2:42 is a church that is devoted to four things:

1. the apostles' teaching
2. and to fellowship
3. to the breaking of bread
4. and to prayer.

The word 'devoted' carries the sense 'attachment like glue'[1] (here's where the glue stick came in). This means that the church members are fixed together, stuck together. When someone joins the church in the biblical sense, they are metaphorically gluing themselves to the apostles' teaching, fellowship, breaking of bread (Communion) and prayer. For many churches, proclaiming and listening to the apostles' teaching, fellowshipping and partaking in Communion is the norm. It's expected. This is what Christians do. But what about prayer – as a church? Glued to prayer? Why?

The daunted disciples gather to pray (Acts 1:13-14)

In the days after Jesus rose victoriously, bodily and world-shatteringly from the grave, He taught His disciples the central theme of Scripture. We read this in Luke 24:45-7:

> This is what is written: The Christ will suffer and rise from the dead on the third day, and repentance and forgiveness of sins will be preached in his name to all nations, beginning at Jerusalem.

What we read here is the good news of Jesus' person, work and mission to the world. And it needs to be understood, proclaimed and lived.

---

1. D. Cook, *Teaching Acts* (Ross-shire, Scotland; Christian Focus Publications, 2007), pp. 81-2.

The good news is:

The Christ: the Greek word for Messiah, the Anointed One – God's chosen King over all the world (as foretold in places such as 2 Sam. 7:14, Ps. 2).

The Christ [who] will suffer – the chosen King over all the world *who would be pierced for our transgressions, crushed for our iniquities; the punishment that brought us peace was upon Him, and by His wounds we are healed* (Isa. 53:5). Here is the sin-bearing, substitutionary sacrifice of Jesus declared. In our place condemned He stood.

The Christ [who] will rise from the dead after three days – the suffering Christ became the triumphant Christ. He is the fulfilment of the words in Psalm 16:10: *because you will not abandon me to the grave, nor will you let your Holy One see decay.* Here is Jesus, the destroyer of both the sting of death, and death itself (1 Cor. 15:54-5).

And repentance… will be preached: all people, in all places, and in all times, are called to confess their rebellion against their Maker and King, acknowledging that their lives are headed (justly) towards death and hell, and call upon God for mercy. Before one can hear the good news of grace, one must first hear the bad news of Romans 1:18 – *the wrath of God is being revealed against all the godlessness and wickedness of men who suppress the truth by their wickedness.*

Once the bad news of rebellion, guilt, imminent death and judgement are fully understood – each person needs to hear the good news of **the forgiveness of sins.** Only the offended can forgive. And if King David was right, that ultimately, *against [God] only have we sinned* (Ps. 51:4),[2] then only God can forgive us. The teachers of the law were correct when they thought: *'Why does this fellow [Jesus] talk like that? He's blaspheming. Who can forgive sins but God alone?'* (Mark 2:7). Here is where the enormity of Jesus' next words can never be overstated: *'But that you may know that the Son of Man has authority on earth to forgive sins…'* (Mark 2:10). Here is God in the flesh – declaring that in Himself, our sins can be forgiven. In Him, can the blessing of Psalm 32:1-2 come to us: *Blessed are they whose transgressions are forgiven, whose sins are covered. Blessed is the man whose sin the Lord will never count against Him.*

This good news is not truly good unless it is proclaimed. And according to Jesus, it **will be** proclaimed. *Repentance and the forgiveness of sins will be proclaimed in His name to all nations.* In these words, we see the summary statement of the Book of Acts, church history, all history leading up to and being consummated in Revelation 7:9-10:

> *After this I looked and there before me was a great multitude that no-one could count, from every nation, tribe, people and language, standing before the throne and in front of the Lamb. They were wearing white robes and were holding palm branches in their hands. And they cried out in a loud voice: 'Salvation belongs to our God, who sits on the throne, and to the Lamb'.*

Heaven itself will never get over the sacrifice of Jesus – and that's why the name that's spoken of Jesus in heaven is predominantly the Lamb! This mission of Jesus will happen, will be completed, because Jesus is the sovereign overseer of this mission.

---

2. What this means is: at the heart of King David's sin against Bathsheba and her husband was rebellion against God. Adultery and murder were the outworking of that rebellion on a social scale.

Finally, Jesus' words in Luke 24:45-7 conclude with the words: beginning at Jerusalem. Here, Jesus' mission will begin – at Mt Zion, the city of David, the location of the triumphant entry of Jesus, and the city gates outside of which Jesus was crucified. Starting here, the prophecy of the Servant in Isaiah would be completed:

> *It is too small a thing for you to be my servant to restore the tribes of Jacob and bring back those of Israel I have kept. I will also make you a light for the Gentiles, that you may bring my salvation to the ends of the earth* (Isa. 49:6).

The question that the Gospels finish with, and the Book of Acts answers, is: how would God's people take His gospel to the ends of the earth? In Acts 1, the scene is set for the onward progress of the redemptive plan of God. And importantly, the scene moves to the upper room (Acts 1:12):

+ the location where Jesus prepared His disciples for His death (Mark 14:15)

+ the location of Jesus' post-resurrection appearance

+ and now, post-ascension, it is the location where the disciples gather again.

Here, in the upper room, as they prepare for the enormous task at hand, what was the first thing they did? The second thing they did was to arrange for a replacement leader for Judas (Acts 1:15-26). But that was not the first thing they did. The first thing the disciples did, after Jesus ascended to His heavenly session, was hold **a 120-person prayer meeting:**

They all joined together constantly in prayer, along with the women and Mary the mother of Jesus, and with his brothers. (Acts 1:13-14).

Here in verse 13 we read of the following people.

+ Eleven apostles who deserted Jesus in the Garden of Gethsemane; who included Peter and his threefold denial of Jesus (who by the time of this prayer gathering had just gone through a threefold restoration to Jesus' mission).

+ These apostles included former enemies, in Matthew (a former tax collector), and Simon (a former Jewish Zealot).

+ Included were Jesus' brothers who once thought Jesus was going out of His mind – but who've been moved from unbelief to belief (John 7:5).

+ Mary and the women who had been on such a profound roller coaster ride – from front row seats to the horror of Jesus' crucifixion, to being the first to see Jesus' resurrection appearances, responding with fear and trembling (Mark 16:8).

It was this motley crew who were tasked with the mission to make disciples of all nations (Matt. 28:18-20). This mission is the largest endeavour the world has known. It still is. And so it makes sense what they do first. They pray! Like this gathering of believers, the church today is made up of a motley crew of people from vastly different backgrounds and experiences, who carry the sense that the Great Commission is overwhelming to the point of hopeless. We are hopeful, yet insufficient. And as people predisposed to task-orientation, we often hear or speak the words: 'you have to do more, be more, step up. The task is huge. It's on our shoulders.' But to act is not our first call.

The believers in Acts 1:13-14 stop, and they pray. The word used to describe their prayer is 'constantly'. Later, Luke describes the early church as devoted to prayer (2:47), and earnest in prayer (12:5).

What is prayer?

The question should now be asked: what exactly is prayer? Prayer can be defined in a number of ways. In its simplest form, it is 'the created capacity to communicate with the Creator'. Or in more relational terms, prayer is the 'personal, conscious awareness and communication with the living and true God'.[3]

The pattern of their prayer was 'keeping of regular hours of prayer (the Jewish hours of prayer), which included the afternoon prayer at 3.00 p.m. (see Acts 3:1; 10:3, 30). But the early church, like Jesus, was not content with restricting prayer to a liturgical form only. Peter prays at noon (10:9), and the Jerusalem church interceded at night for the imprisoned apostle (12:5, 6), while Paul and Silas praise God in prison at midnight (16:25).'[4] They pray because 'prayer is shown to be the means by which God has guided the course of redemptive history, both in the life of Jesus and in the period of the church's expansion.'[5]

This prayer that's grounded in the new covenant, is prayer enabled by the extraordinary access given to

---

3. Stanley Gale, *Warfare Witness* (Ross-shire, Scotland; Christian Focus Publications, 2005) p. 114.

4. See P. T. O'Brien, 'Prayer in Luke-Acts', *Tyndale Bulletin*, 24 (1973), p. 112.

5. O'Brien, 'Prayer in Luke-Acts', p. 112.

Christians – guided by the Scriptures, mediated by God the Son, heard by God the Father.[6]

So the disciples seek power from on high. They need the power that Jesus promised them in Acts 1:8 – the engine room for the rest of Acts.

'But you will receive power when the Holy Spirit has come upon you and you will be my witnesses in Jerusalem, and in all Judea and Samaria, and to the end of the earth.'

In the coming of the Holy Spirit, we come to the fulfilment of the promises of Ezekiel 36:25-8 and Joel 2:28-32:

> I will sprinkle clean water on you, and you will be clean; I will cleanse you from all your impurities and from all your idols. I will give you a new heart and will put a new spirit in you; I will remove from you your heart of stone and give you a heart of flesh. And I will put my Spirit in you and move you to follow my decrees and be careful to keep my laws… you will be my people, and I will be your God.

> And afterwards, I will pour out my Spirit on all people… I will pour out my Spirit in those days… And everyone who calls on the name of the LORD will be saved.

The Messiah has come, lived the life we could never live, died the death we deserve, risen – and is now sending the long-awaited Holy Spirit (the third member of the Godhead). This gift of the Holy Spirit is not a temporary gift as in

---

6. Although prayer is most commonly addressed to God the Father in the New Testament, Alan Thompson convincingly shows that the Lord the disciples pray to in Acts 1:24 is the same Lord referred to in Acts 1:21. That is, the Lord Jesus. Thompson's conclusion is that 'Jesus not only has such authority that He may be prayed to, but Jesus is continuing to direct affairs from "heaven"' (Alan J. Thompson, *The Acts of the Risen Lord Jesus*, NSBT 27 (Downers Grove, Illinois; IVP, 2011), p. 50.

the time of Saul in the Old Testament (1 Sam. 16:14). Now, post Pentecost, He is a permanent gift – to assure, comfort, empower and embolden God's people for service in church and mission. The Holy Spirit is God's power in action. Leon Morris explains it in this way: 'it is plain that the throbbing note of power characterises the Holy Spirit'.[7] Jesus knew that the disciples would be weak. Power from on high would be given so they could be His witnesses (Luke 24:48).

In one of Charles Spurgeon's addresses in *Only a Prayer Meeting*, he poignantly states: 'the coming together of the saints is the first part of Pentecost, and the ingathering of sinners is second. It began with "only a prayer meeting" but it ended with a grand baptism of thousands of converts.'[8]

Prayer for revival

And it should be the model of the present and future church too. Yes, it is the gospel that is the power of God for salvation (Rom. 1:16), but prayer precedes gospel proclamation. This is the model of the early church. And it should be the model of the present and future church too.

Restoring the vertical

The act of prayer, and the subsequent results of our praying, are often a mystery to Christians. How the omnipotent, omnipresent and omniscient God can hear every Christian's prayer, and respond in a timely, God-honouring and people-

---

7. Leon Morris, *Spirit of the Living God* (Belford Square, London; IVP, 1972), p. 17.

8. C. H. Spurgeon, *Only a Prayer Meeting* (Ross-shire, Scotland; Christian Focus Publications, 2000). p. 15.

blessing manner is well and truly beyond us. But the consistent message in Scripture is this: God could choose to work in whatever way He would like – our God is in the heavens; He does whatever He pleases (Ps. 115:3). But He chose to command His people to pray, to hear their prayers, and to respond in His time and His way.

But, as Richard Lovelace wrote in 1979, 'In much of the church's life in the twentieth century, however, both in Evangelical and non-Evangelical circles, the place of prayer has become limited and almost vestigial. The proportion of horizontal communication that goes on in the church (in planning, arguing and expounding) is overwhelmingly greater than that which is vertical (in thanksgiving, confession and intercession).'[9] If we were to be honest, our churches haven't changed too much. This is, of course, a generalisation – but generalisations are often generally true.

Therefore, a clear application of Acts 1 is that 'active planning, strategizing, wise application of good business principles (while all useful), are insufficient for discernment and growth in the church. Prayer to the ascended Christ is essential. A desire to engage in ministry activity must not crowd out prayer.'[10] Have we heard and heeded this? What do our planning meetings tell us? What do our parish council or elders' board minutes tell us? We all want our churches to grow: could it be that *we do not have because we do not ask God?* (James 4:2).

One practical action could be the way we carry out our mid-week 'Bible Studies'. Might it be possible to spend

9. Richard F. Lovelace, *Dynamics of Spiritual Life*, (Downers Grove, Illinois; InterVarsity Press, 1979, p. 153.
10. D. Cook, *Teaching Acts*, p. 62.

time reading the Bible passage, then working through the text carefully, yet briefly, and then spend most of the rest of the gathering praying – asking the God who inspired the Word, to massage that Word deep in us, so that we grow in grasping the grace and knowledge of Jesus with our minds, our emotions and our wills. Could we pray through the Word as much as we study it?

In one of Jesus' parables on prayer (Luke 18:1-5), our Lord showed very clearly what He wants from the church:

> *Then Jesus told his disciples a parable to show them that they should always pray and not give up. He said: 'In a certain town there was a judge who neither feared God nor cared what people thought. And there was a widow in that town who kept coming to him with the plea, "Grant me justice against my adversary."'*

> *'For some time he refused. But finally he said to himself, "Even though I don't fear God or care what people think, yet because this widow keeps bothering me, I will see that she gets justice, so that she won't eventually come and attack me!"'*

Don't give up. Don't stop praying. It is for these reasons that here in Acts 2, we're told the church is devoted to, glued, or stuck to prayer. The church gathered is the church praying. Yes, the early church may well have followed the prescribed Jewish times of prayer – but the motivation wasn't to follow a law, but to be disciplined, always praying, not giving up. There is no prescriptive teaching here – Luke is simply describing what the church does. The church gathers to pray and prays when it gathers. A church that doesn't pray together is a church that has come undone – no longer 'attached like glue' to what is essential. This is a cause for repentance and re-prioritisation.

Reflection Questions

1. How might 'unglued' churches reveal themselves?

2. In what ways does gospel-mindedness lead to prayer-fulness?

3. How might both liturgical and extempore prayer become daily / weekly habits?

4. In what areas do you and your church need to repent and re-prioritise?

3

Prayer – fortified for the mission

(Acts 4:21-31)

One hundred years ago, C. T. Studd famously said: 'Some want to live within the sound of church or chapel bell; I want to run a rescue shop, within a yard of hell.' The sentiment was that the peace and joy of a nice, comfortable life near a nice comfortable church isn't the goal for the Christian. Now is the day of salvation. There is wrath to come, where people face the awful reality of the consequences of life lived in rebellion against Jesus.

We look forward to glory, where the church will be finally and fully the church triumphant. Until then, for all the beauty of Christ's bride on earth, it will remain the church militant. We do battle with powers and principalities, with the roaring lion who seeks people to devour and destroy. There's nothing more dangerous for a church than to be deceived into thinking that we live in a time of peace.

This is the reality the early church found themselves in (Acts 4:21-31). It's the persecuted church in prolonged prayer. This prayer begins with acknowledging the God of the Bible as the Creator and Sovereign ruler of the world (v. 24):

> *On their release, Peter and John went back to their own people and reported all that the chief priests and the elders had said to*

them. When they heard this, they raised their voices together in
prayer to God. 'Sovereign Lord,' they said, 'you made the heavens
and the earth and the sea, and everything in them.'

The God we pray to is absolutely sovereign over all world
events (big or small). The sovereignty of God is not simply
a theological term, but a deeply important reality for our
church life, and mostly for our prayer meetings. If God is
not sovereign, there can be no confidence that the hearer of
our prayers can do anything to help. But God is sovereign,
and He does listen to the prayers of His people. We see this
in Psalm 116:1-2:

> *I love the LORD, for he heard my voice; he heard my cry for*
> *mercy. Because he turned his ear to me, I will call on him as long*
> *as I live.*

Here is confidence. The psalmist prays, 'because God
heard my voice, my cry for mercy… He turned His ear
to me'. Prayer is movement. The movement of the person
or people praying towards God. And it's movement from
God, towards the people praying.

Having begun with this great comfort, the prayer in
Acts 4 moves to Psalm 2, and the reality of the 'raging
nations' that killed Jesus and now attack the early church
(vv. 25-8).

> *You spoke by the Holy Spirit through the mouth of your servant,*
> *our father David: 'Why do the nations rage and the peoples*
> *plot in vain? The kings of the earth rise up and the rulers band*
> *together against the Lord and against his anointed one.' Indeed*
> *Herod and Pontius Pilate met together with the Gentiles and the*
> *people of Israel in this city to conspire against your holy servant*
> *Jesus, whom you anointed. They did what your power and will*
> *had decided beforehand should happen.*

God is still sovereign, even as the church is persecuted. How do they respond? They gather to pray. They bring their circumstances to the One who knows what is happening, and has the power to change things. In summary: 'prayer, then, focussing on the sovereignty of God, sustained by Scripture, is the church's response to hostility'.[1] Do our churches call their members together to pray together when facing trials of any kind? Is that our first response, or is it pragmatic action like financial or food assistance? Before we act, we need to call God's people together for united prayer, together calling upon our Sovereign God for grace, wisdom, and strength to meet the situation at hand.

The Apostle Paul develops our understanding of the role of prayer under persecution in Ephesians 6:18. As Kent Hughes points out in his commentary on this section of Scripture – 'those who would engage in spiritual warfare, regardless of how well they wear truth and righteousness and faith and salvation, regardless of how well they are grounded in peace, regardless of how well they wield the Word, they must make prayer the first work'.[2] And notice, in Ephesians 6:18, this prayer is described as praying in the Spirit. What does this mean? It means that the Holy Spirit directs the prayer, creates the prayer within us, leads us to cry out 'Abba Father' (Rom. 8:14-16), and empowers us to pray and keep praying.[3]

Praying in the Spirit includes all kinds of prayers and requests, on all occasions, praying continually, for all the saints. Planned prayer meetings **and** spontaneous prayer

1. D. Cook, *Teaching Acts*, p. 107.
2. R. Kent Hughes, *Ephesians,* Preaching the Word (Wheaton, Illinois; Crossway, 1990).
3. See D. M. Lloyd-Jones, The *Christian Soldier; An Exposition of Ephesians 6:10-20* (Edinburgh; Banner of Truth Trust, 1977), p. 347.

meetings are the natural outworking of a church that loves God's sovereignty and longs for His intervention in their world.

What is most surprising to many in Acts 4 is that in light of the harsh persecution they faced, the gathered disciples did not pray for protection, nor for judgement on their enemies. Instead, they prayed:

> Now, Lord, consider their threats and enable your servants to speak your word with great boldness. Stretch out your hand to heal and perform signs and wonders through the name of your holy servant Jesus.

For witnesses to Jesus, persecution does not stop the mission, it simply deepens the need to depend on God for power to continue the mission. God's power is available to His people because Jesus is an active participant in His mission. We can see this in the final moments of Stephen's life in Acts 7:55-6:

> But Stephen, full of the Holy Spirit, looked up to heaven and saw the glory of God, and Jesus standing at the right hand of God. 'Look,' he said, 'I see heaven open and the Son of Man standing at the right hand of God'.

Here is Jesus' presence in and over His mission. Although it was Stephen who was on trial for the 'crime' of gospel proclamation (Acts 7:12-13), it was ultimately his listeners who were being held to account. That was the purpose of Stephen's words in Acts 7:51-3. As F. F. Bruce put it: 'Stephen, seeing their hostility and realizing the certainty of an unfavourable verdict, appealed from their judgment to that of the heavenly court, where Jesus stood as witness or counsel for the defence (Acts 7:56).[4] Here is Romans 8:34 in action:

> Who then is the one who condemns? No one. Christ Jesus who died – more than that, who was raised to life – is at the right hand of God and is also interceding for us.

Jesus is the true Judge over all. In Hebrews 12:2 we are told He has sat down, meaning that His work of redemption has been finished. But here in Acts 7:55, Jesus is standing. He's up and He's active. He's participating. He's acting as witness for Stephen. The heavenly court is in session.

I love the encouragement that God gives us through Acts 18:7-11:

> Then Paul left the synagogue and went next door to the house of Titius Justus, a worshiper of God. Crispus, the synagogue leader, and his entire household believed in the Lord; and many of the Corinthians who heard Paul believed and were baptized. One night the Lord spoke to Paul in a vision: 'Do not be afraid; keep on speaking, do not be silent. For I am with you, and no one is going to attack and harm you, because I have many people in this city.'

In verses 7-8, we read of Paul's ministry success – the pure joy of seeing people come to Christ under his gospel proclamation. But then in verse 9, we meet Paul in his weakness. And in Paul's weakness, we are brought into the precious words of the risen Lord Jesus to assure and encourage (give courage to) Paul. Here, the great gospel-proclaimer needs to be encouraged not to be afraid or silent. Why? Because he was afraid and tempted to be silent. So Jesus lifted up Paul's heart and mind to the sovereign Lordship of Jesus over His mission. The result

---

4. See my 'Martyr in Every Sense of the Word', *Churchman*, 125:2 (Summer, 2011), pp. 173-8.

being verse 11 – 'So Paul stayed in Corinth for a year and a half, teaching them the word of God'.

This image of the risen Jesus overseeing His mission to the world, and the prayer meeting which begs for His power for evangelism, is in stark contrast to many church prayer meetings one finds oneself in today. Here, many prayers are given that we might escape trials, be blessed with good health, top marks, job promotions, stress-free days, relaxing holidays etc. 'We tend to pray for circumstances to improve so that we might feel better and life might get better. These are often honest and good requests – unless they're the *only* requests.'[5]

This leads to another great danger that our churches in the West can (and do) constantly fall into: becoming fair-weather Christians. That is, Christians who can only grow and thrive when the going is good. Fair-weather Christians are a stark contrast to Christians who have heard and heeded Jesus' words in John 16:33. *In this world, Christians will have trouble*. That is a given. It's non-negotiable. Many of us in the West are not suffering from violent persecution, but the freeze of the secular humanist culture around us. We are no longer tolerated, but dismissed as irrelevant, even morally harmful. We are facing our time of trouble – relegated to the periphery of society. We are not strong in numbers, influence or reputation. And on top of this, we face trials of health, relationship breakdowns, financial pressure, personal integrity, and much more.

How can we pray? What can we pray for? 'The driving focus of biblical prayer asks God to show himself, asks that we will know him, asks that we will love others.'[6]

---

5. David Powlison, 'Pray Beyond the Sick List', *The Journal of Biblical Counseling*, 23:1, (Winter 2005), p. 5.
6. David Powlison,' Prayer Is a Great Place to Begin Biblical Counseling',

The sheer range of prayers in the Bible highlights the desire of God to be present and active in all aspects of His people's lives. Biblical prayers include presenting God with general hardships, specific pain, confused emotions, overwhelming desires, conflicted relationships, doubted promises, longed for hopes and much, much more. What might praying with this depth and breadth look like in our church?

> When someone asks you, 'How may I pray for you?', imagine the impact of responding in a manner such as this: 'I've had a lot on my mind lately, and have been inattentive and irritable to those nearest and dearest to me. Please pray for me, that I will awaken and turn from my preoccupation with work pressures, recreations, health problems, or money. God promises to help me pay attention to him. Ask him to help me remember and focus. Ask him to help me to take my family and other people to heart. Pray that I will take refuge in Him when the pressure is on. The Lord is my refuge, but I've been taking refuge in TV and food.' This kind of prayer gets things that matter on the table –things that matter both immediately and eternally.[7]

Richard Sibbes famously said, 'it is the poor that doth pray'[8]. He goes on to ask us to 'consider our wants, and our necessity of supply, of our misery in our want, of our hope to prevail by prayer.'[9] In saying 'our wants', he includes personal prayers as well as the local church and global

---

http://www.ccef.org/resources/blog/prayer-great-place-begin-biblical-counseling, accessed 16/05/15.

7. David Powlison, 'Prayer Is a Great Place to Begin Biblical Counseling'.
8. R. Sibbes, *The Works of Richard Sibbes, Vol. VI* (Edinburgh; James Nichol, 1863), p. 167.
9. Sibbes, *Works, Vol. VI*, p.166.

body of believers.[10] It is no surprise that suffering leads to prayerfulness. Suffering is one way that we are led to see our insufficiency and God's all-sufficiency.

Unfortunately, sometimes we get confused as to who is sufficient for the job at hand. David Platt explains,

> When I was considering becoming the pastor of the faith family I now lead, I thought and even said to people, 'This church has so many resources – so many gifts, so many talents, so many leaders, so much money. If this church could get behind a global purpose, it could shake the nations for the glory of God.'
>
> I have since discovered that this was a woefully wrongheaded way to think. The reality is that it doesn't matter how many resources the church has. The church I lead could have all the man-made resources that one could imagine, but apart from the power of the Holy Spirit, such a church will do nothing of significance for the glory of God. In fact, I believe the opposite is true. The church I lead could have the least gifted people, the least talented people, the fewest leaders, and the least money, and this church under the power of the Holy Spirit could still shake the nations for His glory. The reality is that the church I lead can accomplish more during the next month in the power of God's Spirit than we can in the next hundred years apart from His provision. His power is so superior. Why do we not desperately seek it?'[11]

John Newton, in his hymn, 'Come, My Soul, Thy Suit Prepare', wrote 'you are coming to a King. Bring large petitions with thee.'[12] Does the good news of Jesus' person

---

10. The New Testament has surprisingly little reference to individuals praying for themselves. The majority of the New Testament calls to prayer are corporate prayers – prayers that include the person praying, but extend to the Christian community both local and global.

11. David Platt, *Radical* (Colorado Springs; Multnomah Books, 2010), pp. 53-4.

12. John Newton, *Come, My Soul, Thy Suit Prepare* (1780).

and work shape our prayer meetings? If it does, then our prayer meetings will never be boring or uneventful.

The result in the instance of the Acts 4 prayer meeting: '*after they prayed, the place where they were meeting was shaken*'. While they were praying, God manifestly showed His favour on them and their prayers. As well as His favour, His help was supplied in abundance: '*And they were all filled with the Holy Spirit and spoke the word of God boldly*' (v. 31).

The call to boldness is necessary today. In fact, it always has been – because we are so often timid in speech, especially with the possibility of opposition. It's the risen Lord Jesus and the empowering of His Spirit that enables gospel proclamation. And in the process, the truths of 2 Corinthians 4:7 will be made abundantly clear:

> *But we have this treasure in jars of clay to show that this all-surpassing power is from God and not from us.*

Reflection Questions

1. What were your immediate thoughts on the C. T. Studd quote?

2. Do our churches call their members together to pray together when facing trials of many kinds? Should we?

3. How can we pray in trials?

4. What can we pray for?

5. Does the good news of Jesus' person and work shape our prayer meetings?

4

Getting practical – growing as gospellers, bold and clear

Firstly, a warning from J. I. Packer:

> Renewal in all its aspects is not a theme for dilettante debate, but for humble, penitent, prayerful, faith-full exploration before the Lord, with a willingness to change and be changed, and if necessary to be the first to be changed, if that is what the truth proves to require. To absorb ideas about renewal ordinarily costs nothing, but to enter into renewal could cost us everything we have, and we shall be very guilty if, having come to understand renewal, we then decline it. We need to be clear about that. John Calvin once declared that it would be better for a preacher to break his neck while mounting the pulpit if he did not himself intend to be the first to follow God. In the same way, it would be better for us not to touch the study of renewal at all if we are not ourselves ready to be the first to be renewed.[1]

Having heard that warning, if we are still keen to seek large-scale gospel transformation in our churches, cities and world, what could we do?

In Brisbane, the City Bible Forum equips and supports gatherings called Evangelistic Prayer Teams (EPTs). EPTs involve groups of businessmen and businesswomen in the city meeting fortnightly, to pray purely for evangelistic

1. J. I. Packer, *A Quest for Godliness*, pp. 6-7.

opportunities amongst their workmates. They pray for boldness (like the church in Acts 4), and for God to open doors to the gospel and enable them to speak the gospel clearly (Col. 4:5-6).

What might we see as a result of prayer meetings like this? In September 1857, Jeremiah Lanphier, an evangelist in New York City, invited businessmen to a lunch-hour prayer meeting[2]. The purpose: for the gospel of God's grace to capture the hearts and minds of the multitudes outside of Christ in their city and nation. Six people attended the first meeting. The next week, twenty people attended. Then similar prayer meetings were held throughout the city. After a year of these meetings, over 10,000 people were praying daily. They were attended by Christians from churches such as the Methodists, Baptists, Episcopalians, Lutherans, Moravians, Presbyterians, and Congregationalists. The format of the prayer meeting was:

+ Begin with a hymn of praise to God.

+ Read a portion of Scripture (to ground the prayers in the Word of God).

+ Open the floor for prayer requests.

+ Each individual was to pray for no longer than five minutes.

+ No controversial topics to be raised and prayed for – just evangelistic prayer.

People could come and go as they pleased. Five minutes before the hour was up, they sang a hymn and then a pastor delivered a benediction. These prayer meetings then

2. The following report is from Colin Hansen and John Woodbridge's wonderful little book, *A God-Sized Vision*, pp. 77-88.

began in Philadelphia, with 3,000 people gathering to pray weekly there.

The organisers of these prayer meetings sought the unity of Christians in the city – united around the burden to introduce the lost to Jesus Christ. They solicited requests for unsaved family members and distributed evangelistic tracts as people left the meetings. The notes from one meeting stated: 'by conversing with a friend, by inviting him to meet with a Christian minister, by giving him a book or a tract – above all by making him the special subject of prayer in secret, simple as these means appear, they have been all-powerful through the blessing of God to produce the desired result'.

God in His sovereign grace, used these prayer meetings as the precursor to sending forth revival – thousands across America heard the gospel of God's grace in Christ, and were born again into a living hope. The church was built, and the Word continued to increase. And so might it increase in our day – may the knowledge of what God has done in the past spur us on to ask God to do it again!

Evangelistic prayer is also needed for global gospel needs. I have heard of one church planting team having the unofficial motto: 'because people who die without Christ go to hell'. When I first heard this, I found it shocking. But if the words of John 3:36 are true, then the motto is a reflection of reality – a reality that, if fully comprehended, should make us say with Paul, '*I speak the truth in Christ – I am not lying, my conscience confirms it through the Holy Spirit – I have great sorrow and unceasing anguish in my heart. For I could wish that I myself were cursed and cut off from Christ for the sake of my people, those of my own race*' (Rom. 9:1-3). Of course, only Jesus is the curse-bearing

Saviour. But hell is horrible, and we have in our hearts and minds the words of eternal life.

What do we do with this? Richard Lovelace captured the desperate need for prayer when he wrote, 'For those who realistically face the demanding task of local [and global] mission are immediately driven to prayer by the magnitude of the work confronting them.'[3] Some church groups have adopted an unreached or unengaged people group, and pray for them until there is a viable church in that country that is able to reproduce and permeate their society. This might include praying for workers being sent out into the harvest field from our church, or praying for mission agencies who are seeking to reach that country. Once the country becomes 'reached', the church moves to the next group on the unreached list and starts again.[4]

Prayers that could be used in these meetings are:[5]

Pray that many will realise their need of God and will turn to Him in true repentance and faith, and find Jesus Christ as their Saviour and Lord. Pray that great numbers will be born again, into the Kingdom of God.

Pray that the Holy Spirit will convict the world, and your own community, of guilt regarding sin and righteousness and judgement, so that many will turn from sin (John 16:8).

Pray that the community will be less tolerant of sin. Pray that many will see the awefulness [sic] of sin and all its damaging consequences, and turn from their sin in the strength of the One who gives forgiveness of sin and deliverance from sin.

---

3. Lovelace, *Dynamics of Spiritual Life*, p. 152.
4. See *Operation World* or the Joshua Project for more details on unreached people groups.
5. Bill Price, *Enriching your Prayer Life* (Port Macquarie, New South Wales; Theophilus Publishing, 2005), pp. 84-86.

Pray that many will realise the emptiness of life without Him and will find that Jesus Christ gives them life, and life to the full (John 10:10).

Pray that God will be exalted in the view of those in your community who now have no regard for Him.

Pray earnestly for young people, so many of whom are ruining their lives in so many different ways.

Pray that many will repent, give their lives to Jesus and serve Him throughout their lives.

Pray that many will turn from false beliefs, cults, untrue religions, pseudo-Christian cults, materialism, New Age superstitions and all beliefs that keep people enslaved in sin, so that they will find new life in Christ.

Pray that God Himself will restrain and reverse the amazing rise in Satanism and the occult in our community. Pray that He will protect His people from the opposition of Satan. Pray that He will deliver many from this sin into the Kingdom of God.

Pray that Jesus Christ will be lifted up as Saviour and Lord, drawing people to Him.

Pray that preachers will denounce sin, preaching the holiness and justice of God.

Pray that the love of God, and His kindness to us in Christ, will be proclaimed powerfully in the Church through the nation, so that all people may see that our wonderful God is mighty to save.

Pray that wherever the gospel is preached it will be preached in the power of the Holy Spirit, giving life to the spiritually dead.

Above all, **pray** that the Holy Spirit of God will fill many in the church, giving His people holiness, love, concern, power and a burden for those who are living and dying without Christ and without hope.

Pray that God will raise up many young, powerful, dedicated, enthusiastic preachers, with a burning desire to win many lost people for Christ. Pray that they will be filled with the Holy Spirit, to call the nation back to God.

Pray that there will be an expectancy among God's people that He will bless them with a great outpouring of His Spirit.

Gathering for evangelistic prayer was simply what the early church did. Creating opportunities for Christians to gather to pray evangelistically is essential for Bible-believing churches today.

Reflection Questions

1. Why does J. I. Packer think we need warning when it comes to personal and corporate renewal?

2. How might you create an EPT, and with whom?

3. How will you pray for the nations?

4. Pray together.

5

Priorities – God's or ours?

(Acts 6:4)

Thus far in the Book of Acts, it's been quite a ride:

Acts 1: Jesus proclaiming the kingdom of God; giving His disciples their mission to the ends of the earth; His ascension; the prayer meeting and then leadership commissioning.

Acts 2: the coming of the long-awaited Holy Spirit, the Pentecost proclamation and revival, and the formation of the first Christian church (glued to the Word, prayer, Communion and fellowship).

Acts 3-4: healing in Jesus' name, confrontation with opposition, prayer, bold Spirit-filled gospel proclamation, and uncommon generosity and sharing.

Acts 5: the treachery and death of Ananias and Sapphira, the ensuing fear of God, and continued gospel-growth in number and maturity.

Now in Acts 6, the next challenge arises. The problem was social inequity in the church (Acts 6:1-7). Was it a deliberate oversight or was it accidental? We aren't told. The danger: the potential for a significant church split along racial lines (Acts 6:1). The response: a pivotal moment in church history.

What will be the dominant ministry of the church? Will it be social concern or Word-ministry? The answer is given in verses 2-4:

> Brothers and sisters, choose seven men from among you who are known to be full of the Spirit and wisdom. We will turn this responsibility over to them and will give our attention to prayer and the ministry of the word.

The apostles delegate the practical matters to suitable men. As an important aside: church leaders might need to focus here for a moment. The apostles hear the church members' complaints. They actually listen. They don't get defensive (like I've ashamedly been prone to do). They listen to the complaint against the perceived failure of Christian standards. They listen, and they act.

People often think the church cannot change. A comment on a newspaper article about Christians in America having less power in the recent elections went like this:

> Hahahahaha Christians! Your stupid, hate-filled and oppressive superstition is slowly but surely dying! Hahahahahahaha!!!!!!!!

Really? Are we hate-filled and oppressive? Unfortunately, sometimes. Are we dying? No, Jesus is still on the throne overseeing His mission. Is change needed? Often! Is change possible? Thankfully, yes, change is possible.

> Churches can change. Bitterness can be put to death. Fear can be defeated. Compulsions can be broken. Stony hearts can be made soft, and soft words can come from an acid-tongue. People can have power without becoming corrupt. Churches can be places of safety, love and healing. Change is possible

because the King has come, sent His Spirit, and is in the business of change.[1]

And that's what we see in Acts 6. The apostles stop, listen, and act. The conclusion: there must be some members of the church set apart for the ministry of community care. But, and this is a big BUT: there must also be men and women in the church who are set apart for teaching the Bible, and praying for the church and the world. In the words of one church historian, the pressing need for the early church (and for us today!) is: 'the main thing is that the main thing remains the main thing'.[2] The reason for this: it is through the proclamation of the Word that God gives direction and strength to all ministries (including social concern). So the apostles focus on the Word and prayer.

Acts 6:4 is the early church carrying forward Jesus' pattern: a two-pronged ministry of proclamation and prayer.

Shepherding like the Good Shepherd

Jesus' ministry leading up to His passion might be summed up in Luke 5:15-16:[3] *'Yet the news about him spread all the more, so that crowds of people came to hear him and to be healed of their sicknesses. But Jesus often withdrew to lonely places and prayed.'* Peter O'Brien, in his paper on prayer in Luke-Acts,[4] states that 'Luke in his Gospel presents a full picture of Jesus at prayer.' O'Brien then shows how Luke in Acts presents the early church and its individual members,

---

1. Paul David Tripp, *Instruments in the Redeemer's Hands*, (Phillipsburg, New Jersey; P & R Publishing Co., 2002), p. 6.

2. Quoted in Cook, *Teaching Acts*, p. 125.

3. J. Rinne, *Church Elders*, (Wheaton Illinois; Crossway, 2014), p. 111.

4. O'Brien, 'Prayer in Luke-Acts', p. 122.

including apostles, engaging in the exact same, prayerful activity. The picture is developed as we see the (deliberate) parallels between Jesus and the church highlighted.[5]

+ Immediately after His baptism Jesus prays and receives the Holy Spirit (Luke 3:21); the apostles and their companions (Acts 1:14) pray before the descent of the Spirit upon them (2:1-4). At Acts 8:15 Peter and John pray for the Samaritans that they may receive the Holy Spirit. After the apostles lay hands on them the Holy Spirit descends (8:17).

+ Jesus prayed before the choice of the Twelve (Luke 6:12); the early church prays before selecting Matthias (Acts 1:24).

+ Jesus, at the point of His death, prays that His enemies may be forgiven (Luke 21:34), while Stephen, before falling asleep, cries in a loud voice, 'Lord, do not hold this sin against them' (Acts 7:60).

+ And as Jesus offered the 'evening prayer' committing His spirit, in the words of the Psalmist, to the Father's care (Luke 23:46), so the first martyr calls upon the Lord Jesus and cries, 'receive my spirit' (Acts 7:59).

In Acts 6, the response to the apostles' prioritisation of the Word and prayer was: 'this proposal pleased the whole group' (v. 5). It has been noted, 'all Israel's failures resulted from a failure of leadership. Her leaders lost focus on Yahweh and that infected their every decision. Today's

5. O'Brien, 'Prayer in Luke-Acts', p. 122.

leaders must zealously lead with God's priorities. God will honour such leadership.'[6] For our churches, this must mean gospel-centred sermons, but it must mean no less than prayerful leaders who do the work of prayer (privately and publicly).

What was the result of prioritising the Word and prayer in church?

> *So the Word of God spread. The number of disciples in Jerusalem increased rapidly, and a large number of priests became obedient to the faith (Acts 6:7).*

O may this be said of our churches – that hard-hearted opponents of the gospel come to the obedience of faith, as believers gather, as the church gathers, and as servants of both Word and prayer carry out their ministry in season and out of season.

Reflection Questions

1. It is easy to bemoan the state of our church's current environment. Sin is easy to identify. Is there any hope for change? How?

2. What might be the connection between leaders who listen and act upon the requests of their people, and the same leaders' commitment to prayer?

3. What is the result of prioritising the Word and prayer in church? Is this guaranteed?

---

6. D. Cook, *Teaching Acts*, pp. 125-6.

6

Getting practical –'The ministry of word and prayer'

(Acts 6:4)

If there was ever a pastor who is the epitome of Word and prayer, it was the Apostle Paul. How profound was his ministry amongst the Ephesian Church as seen in Acts 20: the mutual love and affection, the commitment to the Word of God's grace, and the humble prayer for the future of the Ephesian Church in Acts 20:36. Churches need the Word of his grace, but they also need the prayers of their pastors. Paul was a true carer of souls, concerned with the eternal condition of his people.[1] Prayer is one of the greatest gifts we can give to the people we are ministering to.

What does pastoral prayer look like? Thankfully, Paul wrote many of his prayers down for us. They are models for pastors/elders to be ministers of Word and prayer. We must move beyond Acts for the moment to see these prayers in detail.

Paul's pastoral prayer for the Colossian Church

We always thank God, the Father of our Lord Jesus Christ, when we pray for you (Col. 1:3).

---

1. D. Cook, *Teaching Acts*, p. 243.

Pastors aren't always quick to give thanks for their congregation. Members aren't always quick to give thanks for their church. Although Paul had never been to the Colossian Church, he had general oversight over the Gentile Churches (Acts 9:15). And the Colossian Church was facing a real danger. They were under pressure from false teachers urging them to move away from Christ, His supremacy and His gospel 'to hollow and deceptive philosophy that depends on human tradition and the elemental spiritual forces of the world' (Col. 2:8). There was much to be concerned about here.

And consider the situation in which Paul found himself while writing this Letter. He was in jail, chained to a soldier, in cramped conditions, and under a likely death sentence. He was languishing in jail, they were free. But his concern was not for himself, but for them.

An old question used to identify personal character is: what happens when you squeeze oranges? Orange juice?[2] Probably, if someone hasn't tampered with it, or squeezed it already. But generally, when you squeeze an orange, what comes out is whatever is inside it. What happens when life 'squeezes' a Christian? What is revealed is whatever is inside. What happens when you're squeezed? What comes out?

Paul was being squeezed by both the Jewish leaders and the Roman Empire. Squeeze Paul, and what do you get? You get thanksgiving, other-person centred joy. 'We *always* thank God.' Ongoing, persistent thankfulness. It was with integrity that Paul could call others to pray *continuously* (1 Thess. 5:17), as this was his practice.

---

2. Joni Eareckson Tada, *Seeking God: My Journey of Prayer and Praise* (Milton Keynes, England; Word Publishing, 1991), p. 20.

The Greek word that Paul uses for thanksgiving (eucharist) has at its core the concept of *charis* (grace). To be thankful is to know the grace of God, having received from God, knowing what was received were gifts (not earnings) and that they can never be repaid. That's why our neediness is central to prayer – why we give thanks, why we pray. The basis of prayer is always the gospel, grace, welcome, invitation to come, ask, seek, knock – with utter confidence. Genuine faith comes from knowing my heavenly Father loves, enjoys, and cares for me. This is genuine faith.

In the words of the poet George Herbert (1593-1633) entitled 'Gratefulness':

> Thou that hast given so much to me,
> Give one thing more, a grateful heart.
> …
> Not thankful, when it pleaseth me;
> As if Thy blessings had spare days;
> But such a heart ,whose pulse may be
> Thy praise.

Paul then moves from ongoing, persistent thankfulness, to ongoing, persistent petition. '*For this reason, since the day we heard about you, we have not stopped praying for you*' (Col. 1:9). That's Paul. And he calls us to do the same. In Colossians 4:12 we read how Epaphras, the former pastor of the Colossian Church, was *always wrestling in prayer for* his flock.

- *Always*: ongoing, persistent, never ceasing.

- *Wrestling*: the word has the image of a wrestler – grappling, combat, face-to-face, intense, tiring. The Puritan Thomas Goodwin pointed out

that 'our fallen nature is actually allergic to God
and never wants to get too close to Him. Thus
our fallen nature constantly pulls us away from
prayer.'[3] We battle with praying, but we also battle
in our praying. Satan is real. Jesus is on the throne
– so we go there (Heb. 4:16).

• *In prayer*: speaking with God; leaning on the Good
Shepherd – the One who can change things.

• *For you*: it's been said that the Colossian Church
was able to stand tall, because Epaphras lived on
his knees.

Day in, day out. Desperate. In prayer for the Colossian
Church. Is this unique, or is it the description of normal
pastoral ministry?

So what sorts of things should church leaders be
praying for those under their care? What did the Apostle
Paul think we most need? The first thing was knowledge.

> *We continually ask God to fill you with the knowledge of his
> will through all the wisdom and understanding that the Spirit
> gives, so that you may live a life worthy of the Lord and please
> him in every way: bearing fruit in every good work, growing in
> the knowledge of God… .*

Here's the pastor's and the church members' number one
need. We need all the understanding and wisdom that
God offers. God knows everything about everything, sees
everything, knows what's happening now, what's going
to come next, what's going to work, what brings human
flourishing, what doesn't. He has it. But we don't. So we
pray for knowledge.

---

3. Quoted in Richard Lovelace, *Dynamics of Spiritual Life*, p. 155.

Thankfully, we have God's Word, the Bible, where the treasures of God's wisdom are found. But having read it isn't enough, we need it massaged into our minds. We need to carry it around within us, hidden in our hearts.

What's the result of receiving God's wisdom and understanding? A life lived *worthy of the Lord, pleasing Him in every way*. A high standard? Yes! We live in a world of people pleasing – where people are big and God is small. But here, it's about re-orienting who we want to please. Praying, asking God to make Himself big (as He is), and people to be small (as they are). It's about living up to God's expectations.

Next to knowledge, Paul's prayer shows that we need **power** (v. 11):

May you be strengthened with all power, according to His glorious might, for all endurance and patience... .

In our everyday lives, in the many things we face each day, each year – we need God's strength. We need the strength of the all-powerful God who loves to give His power to His people. What's this power to bring? Is it money, fame, success in relationships? No, in the first place, it's all about *endurance and patience*. This power isn't for quick fixes, but stamina for the long haul. It's supernatural power – for how to process pain and struggle, love well, battle sin, grow in the fruit of the Spirit – not just for now, or for the following week or month, but for all of life. It is an ongoing prayer, knowing that change is possible. This is at the heart of asking. The God who is infinite, yet personal, calls us to come to Him, asking, seeking, knocking. Paul's prayers were infested with pleading for power. As God gave grace to Paul, Paul extended grace to the Colossians, Corinthians,

Ephesians, Philippians, Romans, Thessalonians, Galatians and beyond.

As Paul Miller says: 'What do we lose when we begin a praying life? We lose control and independence. What do we gain? We gain [a growing] friendship with God, a quiet heart, the living work of God in the hearts of those we love, the ability to roll back the tide of evil. We lose our kingdom and get His. We move from being an independent player to a dependent lover. We move from living as a practical orphan to [living a life lived with the riches of being] a child of God.'[4] Prayer can be summarised as our need + His sufficiency = our all-sufficiency in every circumstance. So are we praying for God's knowledge and power to fill His people in our churches?

It's the gospel that constantly shapes Paul's pastoral prayers. His prayer for the Colossians finishes with

> For he has rescued us from the dominion of darkness and brought us into the kingdom of the Son he loves, in whom we have redemption, the forgiveness of sins.

Then in Ephesians 3:14-21 we read:

> For this reason I kneel before the Father, from whom every family in heaven and on earth derives its name. I pray that out of his glorious riches he may strengthen you with power through his Spirit in your inner being, so that Christ may dwell in your hearts through faith. And I pray that you, being rooted and established in love, may have power, together with all the Lord's holy people, to grasp how wide and long and high and deep is the love of Christ, and to know this love that surpasses knowledge — that you may be filled to the measure of all the fullness of God.

---

4. P. Miller, *A Praying Life*, (Illinois; Navpress, 2009), pp. 125-6.

The joyous knowledge of the power of God is the foundation of this prayer – we are praying to the God who is both good and powerful to act. He is the listening God, and the acting God. And it is the Holy Spirit who is the mediator of that power to His people. And prayer here in Ephesians 3 is for this power to be activated in the inner being of Christians – so that they will grasp the enormity of God's love for them in Christ Jesus. It's a prayer for the Triune God to overwhelm His people's hearts and minds with His overwhelming love. The prayer is needed, because we can speak the truth of the gospel every Sunday and in Bible Studies and in visitations, but it is the Spirit alone who applies the truths so that every impulse of our lives is shaped by Christ's redeeming love. We are powerless to change people. Paul knew this. All pastors know this. That's why we pray, and keep praying.

How our churches need their pastors praying the same for them today. Just imagine if these prayers were applied to the hearts and minds of the people in our congregation.

Charles Spurgeon once said: 'Whitefield and Wesley might preach the Gospel better than I do, but they could not preach a better Gospel!'[5] Paul's prayers teach us the very same thing: there is no better gospel to preach and to pray. Nor will there ever be! And Acts 6:4 calls upon elders/pastors/church leaders to have confidence, and to make time and space to preach and pray this gospel.

And there should be a sense of excitement as we pray with Paul. We sense this as we read Ephesians 3:20-21:

Now to him who is able to do immeasurably more than all we ask or imagine, according to his power that is at work within

---

5. Charles Spurgeon, http://www.spurgeongems.org/vols28-30/chs1665.pdf, p. 2; accessed 03/05/2015.

us, to him be glory in the church and in Christ Jesus throughout all generations, for ever and ever! Amen.

Like the prayers of God's people in Acts 4 – here is Paul filled with great confidence in God. This confidence is grounded in God's sheer sovereignty to bring surprising growth in His people. And the basis of this confidence is the conviction that the power of God is already at work within us. This side of the Day of Pentecost, Christians live with power from on high (Acts 1:8). We do not seek the presence of the Holy Spirit, but the fullness of the Spirit (Eph. 5:18). Part of the pastor's/elders' responsibility is to pray for the power and presence of the Spirit to be made manifest in the lives of their congregation.

Is this what we hear in our congregational prayers? For elders/pastors/leadership meetings – do we know our congregations like Paul did his? And do we spend time praying for our church members, entrusting them to the Word of His grace? Can we wholeheartedly say that we are ministers of the Word and prayer?

How might we go about being ministers of prayer?[6]

1. Public Prayer

Here is a simple model that many have found helpful. It follows the threefold-function of the church as stated in many systematic theologies:[7]

a.   **UP** (worship): asking God's name to be hallowed in and through the life and ministry of our church

---

6. The material in this next section is largely based on Jeramie Rinne's chapter called 'Plead for the Flock' in his *Church Elders*, pp. 113-19.

7. For example, see Wayne Grudem, *Systematic Theology* (Downers Grove, Illinois; IVP, 1994), pp. 867-9.

and members; giving thanks for the manifold gifts of God; and confessing our sins – (1 John 1:9)

b. **OUT** (mission): we ask God to make His name known in the world – praying for the work of the gospel locally and globally, as well as for pressing local/national and world events

c. **IN** (edification): for the needs of our congregation members specifically, praying through the Lord's Prayer, Paul's Prayers – for all our church members, as well as church life in general.

By following this UP/OUT/IN pattern for prayer, we are able to pray in the Spirit on all occasions... with all kinds of prayers and requests... alert and always keeping on praying... for all the Lord's people (Eph. 6:18).

It's probably a good time to call out the elephant in the room. Our church prayer meetings are often discouraging and disappointing. The reality for many churches is that prayer meetings are a neglected ministry, relegated to a select few, and sometimes even abandoned as something that once worked but doesn't anymore. If the thesis of this book is correct – that prayer together is something that Jesus commanded in the Lord's Prayer, the early church modelled, and the apostles made imperative – then how has the prayer gathering gone wrong? Or in other words, how might we be tempted to give up praying – especially as a church? There are many reasons why attendance is poor in our church prayer meetings, whether they are in small groups or large gatherings. Here are some possible reasons:

+ Church members often feel guilty about not praying. Prayerlessness as a church is often not

an intellectual thing – in many churches, people
know the prayer meeting is important. But there
is a disconnection between what we know is
good, and doing it. So the issue of motivation is
important. And here is where we often get stuck
as a church. We can often fall into motivating
people out of guilt. I've often heard it said that
the reason we're not growing is that we're not
praying. This may have truth to it, and guilt for
prayerlessness may be real, but guilt is never the
biblical means for true and lasting change. The
biblical reasons given for praying are the privilege
of communing with the living God whom we can
call Father; the privilege of being in intimate and
transformative relationship with God and one
another; the privilege of having someone we can
give thanks to for every good gift; declaring our
love to our Lord Jesus; casting our individual and
collective burdens on our good and kind God;
praying for His kingdom to come in our family,
friends, neighbours, city, country and world;
asking the Lord of the harvest for more workers to
be raised up and sent out; prayer for healing to the
God who can heal; and many more. If the church
grasped these truths and realities, not just with
their heads but also their hearts, there may be a
profound change to what Spurgeon once cheekily
called 'only a prayer meeting'.

♦   While the above is true, there is sometimes in
some people, a lack of understanding of what
prayer is. A question I've been asked on a number

of occasions is 'if God already knows everything and is totally sovereign in all situations, then why pray?' And why should we pray in groups when we can just pray at home? Will God actually answer these prayers? How? Paul Miller's excellent book 'A Praying Life' gives clear guidance on the why and how of prayer. It would be a helpful first step towards attaching our church and small groups to prayer.

+ Prayer meetings can unfortunately also preserve unhelpful prayer patterns that discourage people from joining in – such as individuals dominating the meetings with long prayers; unfocused prayer is also hard to partner with as they are difficult to follow and therefore difficult to pray along with (prayer doesn't ever need to be worded perfectly, but knowing what you are praying for is often helpful for everyone); showy prayer that seeks to exalt the pray-er and not the God who is being prayed to; one danger that we can often fall into is spending more time on a speaker giving a talk on prayer and/or sharing prayer points than the actual act of praying – this leaves people who want to pray feeling like it was a sharing meeting with prayer tacked on.

+ Sometimes churches can fall into the trap of poorly timed prayer meetings – for example, 6pm on week nights will be very difficult for families to get to.

+ Humanly speaking, it can be discouraging if there's a failure to remember and celebrate the answers to prayer God has given us. We can get so caught up in prayer needs that we forget times of thanksgiving and celebration.

+ Finally, prayer meetings often suffer from a lack of leadership. Prayer doesn't just happen, we need to make it happen – to keep the importance and practical details in the forefront of people's minds. What does a prayer ministry leader's role look like? It could include collating prayer points from church leaders, mission agencies, keeping a journal remembering the previous week's prayer needs and following them up, as well as celebrating answered prayer. Unfortunately, like the danger of welcoming ministry (where we think everyone is a welcomer so we don't need a welcoming team), we often think that it's the role of everyone – but often if it's the role of everyone, it can easily become the role of no one. A prayer ministry leader is a gift to the church – someone who is godly, who loves Jesus and people, who is organised and disciplined, and keeps everyone on track.

2. Elders'/pastoral meetings

Our church leadership meetings need to move beyond simply opening and closing the session with prayer, and then getting to the real business of the meeting. Prayer isn't an aid to the work – it is at the very heart of the work elders do (Acts 6:4). To be ministers of the Word **and** prayer, church leaders need to carve out time to pray – which might include systematically praying through the church membership roll; it might mean having two elders' meetings: one a 'business meeting' and the other a prayer meeting.

Church leaders have limitations of time, energy, knowledge and gifting. And we have a choice to make: what is the best use of our time? As Paul Miller says, 'if you are not praying, then you are quietly confident that time, money and talent are all you need in life. You'll always be a little too tired, a little too busy. But if, like Jesus, you realise you can't do life on your own, then no matter how busy, no matter how tired you are, you will find time to pray.' He goes on to say, 'time in prayer makes you even more dependent on God because you don't have as much time to get things done. Every minute you spend in prayer is one less minute where you can be getting things done doing something "productive". So the act of praying means that you have to rely more on God.'[8]

Personal prayer (one-to-one with other members)

Are our church leaders praying with congregation members? Do our churches see our leaders praying – not showy prayers for human approval or simply to teach how to pray – but real pastoral prayers with and for God's people? If the pastor prays for parishioners he speaks to after the service, might we see church members doing likewise – resulting in little prayer meetings dotted around our buildings and morning teas? How could we begin such a movement? By asking the simple question at the end of a conversation: 'can I pray about this right now?'

Another important aspect of elder/pastoral praying is praying for the sick, which will be covered in chapter 8.

Private prayer

Jeramie Rinne asks the question: 'what would happen in our local flock if Jesus' under-shepherds gave themselves to

---

8. P. Miller, *A Praying Life*, p. 49.

prayer the way they give themselves to budgets, emails and policies?'[9] Could elders/pastors carry around with them the membership list of their church, praying in the car at red lights, on the commute to work, while going for a run? How this would change the life of the elder/pastor, as well as the lives of those being prayed for – because Jesus' throne is the throne of grace, and He is at work, through the prayers of His people, to meet the needs of His needy people.

As the early church modelled their ministry on Jesus' two-pronged ministry of proclamation and prayer, so must the church today.

Reflection Questions

1. What is the relationship between Acts and the New Testament Epistles (Romans, 1 and 2 Corinthians, Galatians etc.)?

2. Why is thankfulness essential, and how can we practise it?

3. How and what did Paul pray for His people? How might we?

4. Pray.

---

9. Rinne, *Church Elders*, p. 119.

7

Prayer – the hallmark of the redeemed

(Acts 9:11)

Following the central ministry of Stephen, his witness and trial, we are to note how the spread of the gospel moves beyond Jerusalem and into Judea and Samaria (Acts 7; 8:1, 4). Jesus' mission is progressing. But it is progressing primarily through persecution. Now, in Acts 9, we get a closer look at the next central character of the book – the dreaded Saul of Tarsus. Saul is commissioned by the Jewish high priest in Jerusalem to carry out a 'Christian eradication plan' in Damascus. He literally had murder on his mind (Acts 8:1).

He's on this mission when he's confronted by the Risen Lord Jesus in Acts 9:1-9. It's an intervention. And it's a world-changing moment – for Saul, and for the world as we know it. Saul is humbled, blinded, and in need of help.

Jesus then (in v. 10) speaks to Ananias, a disciple and target of Saul's rage. He calls him to follow-up the shaken and humbled Saul. Ananias is obviously wary of helping his hater, and says as much in verses 13-14. But Jesus presses on, pushing Ananias forward towards Saul, and in the process gives Saul's future ministry mandate:

This man is my chosen instrument to carry my name before the Gentiles and their kings and before the people of Israel. I will show him how much he must suffer for my name (Acts 9:15-16).

For all Christians today who do not come from a Jewish heritage, it is here that we are to find the key person (behind Jesus) in our spiritual family tree – the Apostle Paul. He is the apostle to us Gentiles.

But in the midst of reading about Saul's future ministry, we can easily miss a key statement of Jesus about basic Christian discipleship. J. C. Ryle profoundly points out, 'when He [Jesus] sent Ananias to Saul in Damascus, He gave him no other evidence of his change of heart than this, "Behold, he prayeth"' (Acts 9:11)[1]

Ryle continued, 'I know that much may go on in a man's mind before he is brought to pray. He may have many convictions, desires, wishes, feelings, intentions, resolutions, hopes and fears. But all these things are uncertain evidences. They are to be found in ungodly people and often come to nothing. In many a case they are not more lasting than the morning cloud, the dew that passes away. A real, hearty prayer, coming from a broken and contrite spirit, is worth all these things put together.[2]

It has been said that Dietrich Bonhoeffer, the German martyr at the hands of the Nazi regime, became a Christian only *after* completing his doctoral studies in theology and having pastored a German speaking church in Barcelona.[3] As a pastor and theologian, Bonhoeffer would have been

---

1. J. C. Ryle, *A Call to Prayer* (Grand Rapids; Baker Book House, 1981), p. 17.

2. J. C. Ryle, *A Call to Prayer*, p. 17.

3. Stuart Coulton, Sydney Missionary and Bible College Newsletter, Winter 2013, Issue 29, p. 2.

expected to know theology (at least intellectually), as well as to live a relatively morally-upright life. What was the difference when he was eventually converted to Christ? His students said that the difference was this: Bonhoeffer started to pray! He admitted that previously, he had never or rarely prayed; but from his conversion on, prayer became a feature of his life. Prayer is a sign of the regenerated life. It is a mark of redemption.

If prayer is a sign and mark of the Christian life – why is it so difficult for so many Christians? The difficulty of prayer is nothing new. Jesus had to teach His disciples to pray (Luke 11:1-4). Again, as stated previously, the Apostle Paul had to continually remind (even command) Christians to pray (1 Thess. 5:17).

As Calvin wrote in a letter to Cranmer, 'On earth we are so poor and famished and yet Christ is seated at the right hand of God. Why, therefore, are we so poor and famished? Because we are lazy and have so little faith to pray.'[4] In response to this ongoing battle with relative prayerlessness, Richard Sibbes points to Daniel's prayer in Daniel 9:18-19 as a model prayer for the church in Sibbes' day. It is very relevant for our day too. It says, 'O Lord, hear, forgive, hearken, do, defer not!' Make us a praying church, Lord! Send forth your Spirit, exalt your Son, do in us what we could never do in our strength!

John Woodhouse, the former Principal of Moore Theological College, Sydney, stated the reason for prayerlessness in this way:

> If our Christianity has become dry and dull and dead, it will be because the Word of God does not occupy the place it should. If our churches have become closed cliques with no

4. J. Calvin, *Letter to Cranmer*, April 1552.

concern for society and the world around us, it will be because the Word of God does not occupy the place it should. If we have become prayer-less, it will be because the Word of God does not occupy the place it should.

It's an important point that Woodhouse makes: prayerlessness is a mark of someone who is not taking the Bible seriously, nor the life God calls us to.[5]

One implication (of the above) for many of our Bible-believing, gospel-declaring churches is a much-needed rebuke. Contrary to prevailing opinion, churches that are strong on sound theology and expository preaching yet are poor in prayer, are not strong churches, but weak. They are weak because there is a distinct lack of trust in God, reliance on God, humility before God.

One minister who grasped this reality was Charles Spurgeon. As he approached the pulpit, Spurgeon used to pray: 'I believe in the Holy Spirit. I believe in the Holy Spirit. I believe in the Holy Spirit.'[6] This was no superstitious ritual, but a deep realisation of his desperate need for the all-sufficient work of the Holy Spirit.

And we see this surprising work of God developed in Acts 12. Having experienced the heights of the Gentile Pentecost, the church is brought down to earth with another phase of persecution. *It was about this time that King Herod* [the grandson of Herod the Great] *arrested some who belonged to the church, intending to persecute them. He had James, the brother of John, put to death with the sword.*

5. John Woodhouse, 'The God of Word', *The Briefing*, (September 1988). http://matthiasmedia.com/briefing/1988/09/the-god-of-word/
6. Quoted in John Stott, *Between Two Worlds* (Downers Grove, Illinois; IVP, 1982), p. 334.

When he saw that this met with approval among the Jews, he proceeded to seize Peter also (Acts 12:1-3).[7]

Jesus' inner circle is attacked: Peter and James were with Jesus at His transfiguration, and at the raising of Jairus' daughter. James was the first of the martyred apostles. Nine more would come. The others would be exiled. The strange thing here is that only one verse is given to James' murder. It took 75 verses to explain Stephen's death – and he wasn't even an apostle, let alone part of the inner circle of apostles. James just one verse. Why? The only answer we can see is Stephen's death was a catalyst for the move of the gospel out of Jerusalem and Judea and into Samaria. James' death had no real effect on the gospel's movement. The gospel spread is the key. We need to keep remembering this as we read Acts.

For Peter and the early church in Acts 12, things looked dark. It's a heightened season of persecution. There's emphasis on the security assigned to him. Squads of soldiers (v. 4); soldiers, chains and sentries (v. 6); two lines of guards and an iron gate (v. 10). Peter's a prize catch.

But, and it's a big but – there is a hint of hope. In verse 5 we read the church was 'earnestly praying to God for him' (v. 5). Unfortunately, Luke does not record the specific request(s) directed to God, though he does indicate that the intercession was continuous and earnest (v. 5).[8] God, in His sovereign grace, hears their prayers – and miraculously rescues Peter from prison.

Peter then heads straight for the prayer meeting (v. 12). What a triumph this meeting will be! What encouragement

---

7. There is something loathsome about the Herodian Kings. Herod the Great ordered mass infanticide to try and kill baby Jesus.

8. O'Brien, 'Prayer in Luke-Acts', pp. 123-4.

and joy at answered prayer! Unfortunately, no. Strikingly, the very church that is praying for Peter's deliverance is the church who comprehensively disbelieves the news that God has answered their prayers (v. 15). They go as far as saying that it's more likely to be Peter's angel than Peter!

What do we make of this? We are to see this profound truth: God is so gracious that He answers unbelieving prayer.[9] It is not primarily the amount of faith we have, but who we have faith in that counts. The church may have been surprised with God's response to their prayers, but they still prayed. How was Peter set free? Because the church was earnestly praying to God for him.

Acts 12 begins well for Herod. The Jews are onside. The Christian leadership is contained, even decimated. But the church was praying. At the time of war between Protestants and Catholics in Britain, Mary, the Catholic Queen of the Scots, famously said: 'I fear John Knox's prayers more than an army of ten thousand men.' Prayers had healed the sick. Prayers had raised the dead. Prayers had led to the conversion of thousands.

Do we believe that God still answers prayers? We may in theory, but does our practice affirm or deny this? Have we lost sight of who it is we are praying to? Has our God become too small?

How might we get back on track? How might we live out our privileged position to approach God's throne of grace with confidence, drawing near to God (Heb. 4:16, 10:1)? I've found the following account of Dr J. Sidlow Baxter's story personally very helpful. It highlights the centrality of prayer in the life of the Christian, as well as

---

9. D. Cook, *Teaching Acts*, p. 175.

the battle to actually pray. The context was Baxter sharing from his diary with a group of pastors:[10]

He began by telling how in 1928 he entered the ministry determined that he would be the 'most Baptist-Methodist' of pastors, a real man of prayer. However, it was not long until his increasing pastoral responsibilities, administrative duties, and the subtle subterfuges of pastoral life began to crowd prayer out. He began to get used to it, making excuses for himself.

Then one morning came a crisis, as he stood over his work-strewn desk and looked at his watch. The voice of the Spirit was calling him to pray, but at the same time another velvety little voice told him to be practical and get his letters answered, that he ought to face up to the fact that he wasn't the spiritual sort, that only a few people could be like that. That did it! 'That last remark', said Baxter, 'hurt like a dagger blade. I could not bear to think it was true.' He was horrified by his ability to rationalise away the very ground of his ministerial vitality and power.

That morning Sidlow Baxter took a good look into his heart, and he found that there was a part of him that did not want to pray and yet a part that did. The part that didn't was his emotions, and the part that did was his intellect and will. This analysis paved the way to victory. In Dr Baxter's own inimitable words:

> As never before, my will and I stood face to face. I asked my will the straight question, 'Will, are you ready for an hour of prayer?' Will answered, 'Here I am, and am quite ready, if you are.' So Will and I linked arms and turned to go for our time of prayer. At once all the emotions began pulling the other

10. Kent and Barbara Hughes, *Liberating Ministry from the Success Syndrome* (Illinois; Crossway, Wheaton, 2008), pp. 78-81.

way and protesting, 'We're not coming.' I saw Will stagger just a bit, so I asked, 'Can you stick it out, Will?' and Will replied, 'Yes, if you can.' So Will went, and we got down to prayer, dragging those wriggling, obstreperous emotions with us. It was a struggle all the way through. At one point, when Will and I were in the middle of an earnest intercession, I suddenly found one of those traitorous emotions had snared my imagination and had run off to the golf course; and it was all I could do to drag the wicked rascal back. A bit later I found another of the emotions had sneaked away with some off-guard thoughts and was in the pulpit, two days ahead of my schedule, preaching a sermon that I had not yet finished preparing!

At the end of that hour, if you had asked me, 'Have you had a "good time"?' I would have had to reply, 'No, it has been a wearying wrestle with contrary emotions and a truant imagination from beginning to end.' What is more, that battle with the emotions continued for between two and three weeks, and if you had asked me at the end of that period, 'Have you had a "good time" in your daily praying?' I would have had to confess, 'No, at times it has seemed as though the heavens were brass, and God too distant to hear, and the Lord Jesus strangely aloof, and prayer accomplishing nothing.'

Yet something was happening. For one thing, Will and I really taught the emotions that we were completely independent of them. Also, one morning, about two weeks after the contest began, just when Will and I were going for another time of prayer, I overheard one of the emotions whisper to the other, 'Come on, you guys, it's no use wasting any more time resisting: they'll go just the same.' That morning, for the first time, even though the emotions were still suddenly uncooperative, they were at least quiescent, which allowed Will and me to get on with prayer un-distractedly.

Then, another couple of weeks later, what do you think happened? During one of our prayer times, when Will and I were no more thinking of the emotions than of the man on the moon, one of the most vigorous of the emotions unexpectantly sprang up and shouted, 'Hallelujah!' at which all the other emotions exclaimed, 'Amen!' And for the first time the whole of my being – intellect, will and emotions – was united in one, cooordinated prayer-operation. All at once, God was real, heaven was open, the Holy Spirit was indeed moving through my longings, and prayer was surprisingly vital. Moreover, in that instant there came a sudden realisation that heaven had been watching and listening all the way through those days of struggle against the chilling moods and mutinous emotions; also that I had been undergoing necessary tutoring by my heavenly Teacher.

Reflection Questions

1. Why was Saul praying in Acts 9:11 so significant?

2. How was this expressed in Dietrich Bonhoeffer's life?

3. What has laziness and unbelief to do with prayer-lessness?

4. Discuss the quote from John Woodhouse. Is it valid? Why? Why not?

5. How could your church be strengthened? Think concretely.

8

Prayer for healing – the what and how

(Acts 9:36-42)

*How long O Lord? Will you forget me forever? How long
will you hide your face from me? How long must I wrestle
with my thoughts and day after day have sorrow in my heart?
How long will my enemy triumph over me? Look on me and
answer, Lord my God (Ps. 13:1-3)*

It has surprised many a Christian to learn that there are
more psalms of lament than praise. It certainly surprised
me. Honest emotion – a life lived in touch with reality.
God-honouring, yet God-searching prayer in the midst of
trials. Lamenting has been said to be a lost art for many
Christians today. But for many, praying lament is easier
than praying for healing.

We read James 1:2 and wrestle to consider 'trials as
pure joy'. We rightly celebrate the Christ-likeness of people
such as Joni Eareckson Tada – who has experienced life
in a wheelchair as her passport to joy. But what do we
do with passages such as Acts 9? Couched in between
the conversion of Paul (Acts 9:1-31), and what has been
termed the Gentile Pentecost (Acts 10), are two profound
little stories of healing (Acts 9:32-42).

1. The first is the healing of Aeneas, a paralytic who had been bedridden for eight years (v. 33).

2. The second is the healing of Tabitha. Her healing will be the focus of this chapter. We find it in Acts 9:36-42.

In Joppa there was a disciple named Tabitha (in Greek her name is Dorcas); she was always doing good and helping the poor. About that time she became sick and died, and her body was washed and placed in an upstairs room. Lydda was near Joppa; so when the disciples heard that Peter was in Lydda, they sent two men to him and urged him, 'Please come at once!'

Peter went with them, and when he arrived he was taken upstairs to the room. All the widows stood around him, crying and showing him the robes and other clothing that Dorcas had made while she was still with them.

Peter sent them all out of the room; then he got down on his knees and prayed. Turning toward the dead woman, he said, 'Tabitha, get up.' She opened her eyes, and seeing Peter she sat up. He took her by the hand and helped her to her feet. Then he called for the believers, especially the widows, and presented her to them alive. This became known all over Joppa, and many people believed in the Lord.

Tabitha was a faithful Christian woman. She became sick and she died. The church heard that Peter was nearby – so they called for him. What they expected from him is unknown. But Peter, in his usual straightforward manner, went to the house where her body was, sent all the mourners out of the room, got down on his knees, and prayed. What result Peter expected from his prayers we don't know. But, in close parallel to Jesus and Jairus' daughter (Mark 5:41), Peter spoke to the deceased Tabitha and told her to get up, which she did (this is all related very matter of factly!).

It's a profound story. What do we do with such a miraculous event? It's a simple healing – no medical follow-up required.[1] For many, Acts is (rightly) seen as a unique time in redemptive history. The gospel is attested to with signs and wonders many of us in the West today are unfamiliar with.

And, as all people who are intimately involved in the lives of others know, sickness and health, healing and ongoing suffering is a deeply sensitive issue. As I shared in the introduction, I have spent much of my life battling mental illness. I know the dark depths of emotion that the psalmist in Psalm 88 experienced. I know the despair of overwhelming anxiety, to the point of being repeatedly physically sick.

In a moment of panic as a teenager, I remember riding my bike around our neighborhood, peddling faster and faster in an attempt to get intrusive thoughts of self-loathing and fear out of my head. Unfortunately, this attempt failed to bring about the desired result. So I moved to plan B: prayer. I didn't have a clear understanding of who God is – but felt that there was a God, and out of sheer exhaustion I cried out for mental healing. I called and called upon God to be merciful. But I had no confidence God would answer. Although I had a loving family to lean on constantly, in the darkness of my mind I felt what seemed like the indifference and purposelessness of the world around me to my hurt. Richard Dawkins explains this well in these words:

---

1. I find it surprising that F. F. Bruce seemingly agrees with the statement of W. K. Hobart: 'The circumstantial details of the gradual recovery of Tabitha are quite in the style of medical description' (see Bruce, *The Book of the Acts*, Grand Rapids, Michigan; Eerdmans, 1988). There is no hint in the text of a gradual recovery – Tabitha was dead, then alive, then presented to all the believers.

Nature is not cruel, only pitilessly indifferent. This is one of the hardest lessons for humans to learn. We cannot admit that things might be neither good nor evil, neither cruel nor kind, but simply callous – indifferent to all suffering, lacking all purpose.[2]

An indifferent world. A purposeless plight. A fearful future. Helpless. However, when I was twenty-one, God in His inexhaustible grace opened my eyes to His reality. He did this by showing me the glory of His Son, His cross and resurrection, my sin and the gift of His Spirit. Illumination of the gospel truths brought the regeneration of my heart and mind, which brought me trembling-yet-confident of the Father's welcome of me as His child. Everything changed. Prayer moved from an exercise of despair to a relational act of love and hope. The true and good God of this world is the God of Psalm 116 – who turns His ear to His children. God is the God of active listening at its best.

Since then, I have had the privilege of being in churches that know and love this God, who trust that He is both good and strong. And in these churches, I have been anointed with oil by church leaders. I have been encouraged to confess the sins that have gripped my heart. I have been prayed over - with no full (mental) healing, but healing nonetheless: the peace of God has gripped my soul, deep and lasting. And this inner healing has flowed on – in reconciled relationships and comfort to others (2 Cor. 1:3-8), and profound witnessing opportunities. I've seen others healed; I've prayed for their healing, received confidence that prayer is answered – that the exact prayer we prayed was answered. The exhilaration! Praise God!

---

2. *River Out of Eden: A Darwinian View of Life* (London; Weidenfeld & Nicolson,1995), p. 112.

Let's step back for a moment. A question that every Christian has to face at some point or other is: how am I to understand myself in this world? We are 'present-tense' sinners, like Paul (1 Tim. 1:15). And at the very same time, we are saints (1 Cor. 6:11). How does this work? The old Latin phrase 'Simul iustus et peccator' sought to acknowledge these two realities. We are at the same time both righteous and a sinner. We are sinners who've been forgiven, cleansed, and made right in God's sight (Titus 3:3-7). But where does suffering come into this? Michael Emlet helpfully adds a third category: sufferers. He writes: 'Scripture assumes that, since the fall, the people God has chosen are sufferers.'[3]

This is helpful, because it enables our ministry to others to be specific – to encourage the saints, to comfort the suffering, or to confront sin. Sometimes suffering has nothing to do with our sin. But at other times, suffering is the direct consequence of our sin.

How do we apply the Word and prayer to the specific details of the suffering of God's people? What might this look like?[4] Acts 9:28 is James 5:13-16 in action – the church taking responsibility for the sick and hurting, and the leaders of the church praying for healing. We see one answer in James 5:14. Is any one of you sick? He should call the elders of the church to pray over him and anoint him with oil in the name of the Lord.

---

3. Michael R. Emlet, *Cross Talk* (Greensboro, North Carolina, New Growth Press, 2009) p. 76.
4. The rest of this chapter has been significantly influenced by a sermon on James 5 by Pete Ko (pastor at South West Chinese Christian Church, Sydney), as well as John Piper's sermon on James 5 found at: http://www.desiringgod.org/sermons/the-elders-the-people-and-the-prayer-of-faith

Firstly, who are elders? They're proven and godly men appointed to lead over the church. Why elders? Elders represent the church and have the God-given ministry of the Word and prayer (Acts 6:4, 1 Tim. 3:1-7, Titus 1:5-9). So, when the elders are called to pray, it's representatively calling for the whole church to be behind this request. The ministers of Word and prayer pray for healing.

But so as not to restrict healing prayer solely to elders, we read in James 5:16: 'pray for each other'. This refers to the church in general. The gathered church is a praying church, including prayer for healing.

Anointing with oil has been a practice of the church (in many different denominations) since the days of the early church. James 5:14 gives the biblical grounds for this practice. What is the purpose of the oil? In James 5, there's no evidence that this is referring to special anointing oil. It is just oil. But the oil is symbolic. In the Old Testament, oil was a symbol of setting someone apart – e.g. kings and priests (Lev. 8:10, 1 Sam. 16:13). Therefore, the function of oil and anointing the sick with oil, is symbolically setting the sick person apart for God's special attention.

Apart from the above reason for anointing a church member with oil, there is something profoundly pastoral in the act of touch as well as prayer. The touch of compassion and care is thoroughly Christ-like. Jesus often healed people with just a word, but on a number of occasions, he physically touched the person and healed them (Mark 8:25). In the case of the leper in Mark 1:41, the touch was entering into the very plight of the alienated and isolated man. It was an incredible act of grace. It is the privilege of the pastor/ elder to (appropriately) enter into the joy of this personal ministry.

And now for the most difficult bit of this passage: James 5:15 – *And the prayer offered in faith will make the sick person well; the Lord will raise him up.* What's difficult here is the level of certainty: it will happen. As a pastor, I have on a number of occasions anointed church members with oil for a whole range of afflictions, and though I have seen people's lives changed, none have been healed instantly. How does this confidence in healing work? We know from Acts 28:8 that Paul's prayer healed Publius' father. But we also know from Scripture that not all sicknesses are healed.

- 2 Timothy 4:20: Paul left Trophimus sick in Miletus.

- 1 Timothy 5.23: Timothy had frequent illnesses.

- Philippians 2:27: Epaphroditus was ill and almost died.

These men were all with Paul, through whom lots of miraculous healings (and even raising of the dead) were performed! Why weren't they healed? We have to stop here and say, we don't know. We know sometimes God chooses to heal, and sometimes He doesn't. This would be very hard to process, except for the knowledge from the Scriptures that God is sovereign, good and loving. The character of Christ, the depths of His experience of our pain and shame, and His gospel of grace, allow us to put our people in His hands, knowing that He is their Good Shepherd.

The next question must be: what is the place of our faith in prayer? Faith does have something to do with the certainty of healing. But we need to notice in James 5:15 that it's not about the faith of the sick person, but the faith of the people praying (the elders). This tells us that we can't blame the sick for their lack of faith. And again, the important thing about faith is the object. Faith is confidence in God. In this case: faith in the God who heals and the God who sometimes mysteriously (to us) doesn't heal. Oswald Chambers explained this by saying: 'Faith for my deliverance is not faith in God. Faith means, whether I am visibly delivered or not, I will stick to my belief that God is love. There are some things only learned in a fiery furnace.'[5]

But we need to go back to the question: but Peter healed Tabitha, and James 5 says there is certain healing – they will be healed! What do we do with this? Can we have certainty? How? This is a big question for church leaders, and those who call upon the elders to pray for them. John Piper suggests that it has to do with the words 'prayer of faith'. This is something like when God grants a person a kind of gift of faith, which brings a certainty in their heart that as they are praying, the healing will happen. We see this very thing in Peter telling Tabitha to 'get up'. Here is absolute confidence, certainty in healing.

The question is then: how would we know what this prayer of faith is and know the difference? Douglas Moo explains, 'the faith exercised in prayer is faith in the God who sovereignly accomplished His will. When we pray, our faith recognizes, explicitly or implicitly, the overruling providential purposes of God. We may at times be given insight into that will, enabling us to pray with absolute confidence in God's plan to answer as we ask.'[6] The implications for this are: we might experience the prayer of faith only when we as individuals and as a church do

---

5. O. Chambers, 'Run Today's Race', *Christianity Today*, Vol. 31, no.17.
6. Douglas D. Moo, *The Letter of James* (Leicester; IVP, 2000), p. 244.

this lots and lots: pray for one another for sickness and for anything. We have nothing to test it against if we are not a church that's always on our knees in prayer.

When we first planted a church in 2009, I remember asking God to lead some gospel-driven, sound and skilled people to join and serve with us. Instead He sent two young men with drug-problems, one on parole for a violent crime. What do we do in the church with messy, time-consuming people?

A question that needs to be asked of church leaders is: do we take responsibility for the sick and hurting? Do our churches have the culture of the sick and hurting inviting the church leaders to come and pray for them? This takes personal trust from the church members towards church leaders – trust that pastors like Paul won by sharing not just the gospel with his flock, but also his life (1 Thess. 2:8).

Reflection Questions

1. Why should we have confidence to pray for healing?

2. What might prevent people from praying for another's healing?

3. What's your first reaction to the Richard Dawkins quote? What might it be like to live in 'this' world?

4. How does the saint, sufferer and sinner understanding of humanity help us think through hard things?

5. Have you ever been prayed for in the James 5 manner? If yes, explain.

6. Do our churches take responsibility for the sick and hurting? How might we?

9

The church in prayer for its leaders

(Acts 13:1-3; 14:21-3)

When people asked the secret of his flourishing ministry, Charles Spurgeon replied, 'My people pray for me. Let me have your prayers, and I can do anything! Let me be without my people's prayers, and I can do nothing.'[1] Spurgeon could have attributed his success to his grasp of the Scriptures, powerful voice, administrative gifts, organisational systems and support staff. But it was his people's prayers that he most valued, and saw as the strength for his ministry. Here is Spurgeon again on the necessity of prayer for gospel ministers:[2]

+ Everyone who has a work to do for Christ needs the prayers of his fellow Christians, therefore I urge you all to ask for them.

+ However limited may be your sphere, you will not get on without the supplication of others.

+ I crave, beyond all things, your constant prayers.

---

1. C. H. Spurgeon, *The Metropolitan Tabernacle Pulpit*, 63 vols., The Charles H. Spurgeon Library Ver. 2 (n.p, 1865; reprint, Albany, Oregan: AGES Software, Ver. 1.0, 1997), 11:290.
2. Spurgeon, *Only a Prayer Meeting*, pp. 138-9.

+ Here is a way in which you can really help, substantially help, wonderfully help; and this you can do even if you should become bedridden, you could even lie still, and invoke a blessing from God upon our ministry… . Amazing things lie within the reach of the believing man [or woman]. 'All things are possible to him that believeth.'

Do pastors, church leaders, and missionaries today know and experience these blessings? Are we asking for them?

In Acts 9, the Apostle Paul is converted to Christ and named by Jesus as the missionary to the Gentiles (Acts 9:15). Then in Acts 10 Peter preaches to the Gentiles and many are redeemed. The gospel is being proclaimed to Jerusalem, Judea and Samaria. Paul has been set apart for this ministry, but it is in Acts 13:1-3 that Paul begins this ministry officially. We read:

> Now in the church at Antioch there were prophets and teachers: Barnabas, Simeon called Niger, Lucius of Cyrene, Manaen (who had been brought up with Herod the tetrarch) and Saul. While they were worshiping the Lord and fasting, the Holy Spirit said, 'Set apart for me Barnabas and Saul for the work to which I have called them.' So after they had fasted and prayed, they placed their hands on them and sent them off.

In Acts 9, it was Jesus who set apart Paul for the Gentile mission. Now it is God the Holy Spirit identifying Paul (and Barnabas) for this ministry (v. 2). The response of the church is prayer and fasting. Peter O'Brien shows the importance of prayer in the Antioch Church with these words:

> God's revelation concerning the important Gentile mission was given to a church at prayer; their missionaries had been released

with prayer and fasting, and their whole work had been given over
to God's grace in prayer. One further point needs to be added in
connection with prayer and the expansion of the church in Acts.
If the beginnings of the congregations in the Gentile mission were
due to God's activity, and the appointment and commissioning of
office-bearers were integrally related to petitionary prayer so that
such persons had been commended to God's grace, it was no less
true to say that the continuance of these congregations was due to
God's gracious help given in answer to petition.[3]

Prayer is not a tack-on to the selection and sending of
gospel workers. Mission begins and continues with the
church in prayer. It's Matthew 9:38 in action:

> *The harvest is plentiful but the workers are few. Ask the Lord of*
> *the harvest, therefore, to send out workers into His harvest field.*

It's an interesting thing that those who are to pray in
Matthew 9:38 are the very ones whom Jesus sends out in
the very next verse (Matt. 10:1). The church prays for more
gospel workers, and then members of that same church go.
That's what we see in Acts 13:1-3.

But it's not just the sending that counts. Paul was
prayed for in his 'commissioning service', and he kept asking
for prayer. We see this in Romans 15:30.

> *I urge you, brothers and sisters, by our Lord Jesus Christ and*
> *by the love of the Spirit, to join me in my struggle by praying to*
> *God for me.*

Bruce Dipple explains:

> He doesn't ask them to pray for him. He doesn't ask them to
> pray for his struggle, as if they were onlookers watching it all
> happen. He asks them to join in his struggle. He sees those
> who pray as insiders who join with him in his struggle. Here,

---

3. O'Brien, 'Prayer in Luke-Acts', pp. 125-6.

in Romans 15:30, 'he has no hesitation putting the work of the Holy Spirit and their prayers in the same phrase.'[4]

Are our churches praying for God's Kingdom to come – in our own lives, churches and the world around us? What might this look like? One living example of mission prayer can be seen in the ministry of James O. Fraser – the missionary to the Lisu people of China in the early twentieth century. His ministry began with setback after setback. His struggle during his first years in China showed him many lessons that helped him over his years among the people. Village after village that Fraser ministered in was a closed door. The gospel proclamation was clear, but the soil was unreceptive. Hearts were hard. What was the way forward?

Fraser wrote home to Great Britain, to call upon his supporters to pray. These are his words:

'I will not labour the point. You will see from what I am saying that I am not asking you just to give "help" in prayer as a sort of sideline, but I am trying to roll the main responsibility of this prayer warfare on you. I want you to take the burden of these people upon your shoulders. I want you to wrestle with God for them. I am feeling more and more that it is, after all, just the prayers of God's people that call down blessing upon the work, whether they are directly engaged in it or not. Paul may plant and Apollos water, but it is God who gives the increase; and this increase can be brought down from heaven by believing prayer, whether offered in China or in England. We are, as it were, God's agents – used by Him to do His work, not ours. We do our part, and then can only look to Him, with others, for His blessing. If this is so, then Christians at home can do as much for foreign missions as

4. Bruce Dipple, *Becoming Global* (Croydon, SMBC Press, New South Wales; 2011), p. 37.

those actually on the field. I believe it will only be known on the Last Day how much has been accomplished in missionary work by the prayers of earnest believers at home… . Solid, lasting missionary work is done on our knees. What I covet more than anything else, is earnest, believing prayer, and I write to ask you to continue in prayer for me and the work here.'[5] Here we see the equal importance of senders and goers.

But if the church was all about sending workers out, who would oversee the church at home? Who will lead the church? And how will they be best prepared for service, and cared for in that service? We see the answer to this in Acts 14:

+ Paul and Barnabas, having been sent by the Antioch Church in Acts 13, preached throughout the region of Galatia – Psidian Antioch, Lystra and Iconium (Acts 14:21).

+ God brought many people into His kingdom through this gospel preaching (Acts 14:48; 14:1; 14:21).

+ The churches then gathered and leaders were set apart who would oversee each church (Acts 14:23).

+ It is in this setting that we see how church leaders are commissioned. 'Paul and Barnabas… with prayer and fasting, committed them to the Lord' (14:23).

Appointing church leaders can easily become a man-made process. Gifts, character and vision are searched for and

5. Taken from James O. Fraser's Journals, https://omf.org/us/the-prayer-of-faith/ accessed 31/5/15.

found. Leaders are noticed, equipped and set apart. These aspects of a leader are important. But nothing is more important for a church's future than ministers of the gospel who are prayed for at their ordination, and continue to be prayed for. According to Acts, appointment to and ministry in specific tasks are bound up with petitionary prayer.[6]

Prayer was the desperate need of the church leaders in Acts 14, and it still is for church leaders today.

What do leaders need prayer for? :

+ The proclamation of the Word (2 Tim. 4:1-5).

+ The discipline of prayer for the church as a whole and the members of the church as individuals (2 Thess. 5:16-18).

+ Holiness of life: character (1 Tim. 4:16). Or in the words of Robert Murray McCheyne: 'A holy minister is an awful weapon in the hand of God.'

+ If they are married, then a godly, growing and gracious marriage relationship – marked by Christlike love, commitment and joy (Eph. 5:22-33; 1 Tim. 3:1-7).

+ If they are parents, then to be present for their children, to bring them up in the instruction of their good Lord (Eph. 6:4), to see their children as a gift and not a project (Ps. 127:3-5), to shepherd their heart and be a safe person of trust and counsel.

+ For their physical and psychological health: Paul's mental anguish and anxiety for the church/es, Timothy's regular stomach ailments.

---

6. O'Brien, 'Prayer in Luke-Acts', p. 125.

- For their partnership with co-workers: see Paul and John Mark (Acts 15:36-40), and the reconciling, nurturing ministry of Barnabas (Acts 9:26-8).

- For their work as an evangelist (1 Tim. 4:5).

- For friendship: Paul's close relationship with Timothy. Hebrews 3 – under God, we are both needed and needy.

- For Bible passages, see Mark 10, Colossians 4, 1 Timothy 3, Titus 1, 2, Timothy 4, 1 Peter 5.

Here is a prayer from *The Valley of Vision*, entitled A Minister's Preaching.[7] How preachers would love congregation members praying this prayer on their behalf:

My Master God,
I am desired to preach today,
but go weak and needy to my task;
Yet I long that people might be edified with divine truth,
that an honest testimony might be borne for thee;
Give me assistance in preaching and prayer,
with heart uplifted for grace and unction.
Present to my view things pertaining to my subject,
with fullness of matter and clarity of thought,
proper expressions, fluency, fervency,
a feeling sense of the things I preach,
and grace to apply them to men's consciences.
Keep me conscious all the while of my defects,
and let me not gloat in pride over my performance.
Help me to offer a testimony for thyself,
and to leave sinners inexcusable in neglecting thy mercy.

---

7. Arthur Bennett, *The Valley of Vision*, (Edinburgh; The Banner of Truth Trust, 1975), p. 348.

Give me freedom to open the sorrows of thy people,
and set before them comforting considerations.
Attend with power the truth preached.
and awaken the attention of my slothful audience.
May thy people be refreshed, melted, convicted, comforted,
and help me to use the strongest arguments
drawn from Christ's incarnation and sufferings,
that men might be made holy.
I myself need thy support, comfort, strength, holiness,
that I might be a pure channel of thy grace,
and be able to do something for thee;
Give me then refreshment among thy people,
and help me not to treat excellent matter in a defective way,
or bear a broken testimony to so worthy a redeemer,
or be harsh in treating of Christ's death, its design and end,
from lack of warmth and fervency.
And keep me in tune with thee as I do this work.

The missionary un-prayed for is a neglected missionary. Likewise, the pastor un-prayed for is a neglected pastor. Our churches need to be made aware of this – and time needs to be set apart for the church to pray for its pastor/s and gospel workers.

Reflection Questions
Instead of reflection questions for this chapter, spend some time praying for your church leaders as well as missionaries your church supports.

10

People who pray are prepared for anything

(Acts 16:13, 16, 25)

The movement of the gospel from Jerusalem to Judea to Samaria to the ends of the earth is the mission unstoppable: *So the churches were strengthened in the faith and grew daily in numbers* (Acts 16:5). It's the Word of the gospel that grew the church, but it was clearly the Holy Spirit who directed the movement. We see in Acts 16:6-7 that Paul and his mission team were prevented from preaching the Word in the province of Asia and Bithynia. The door was shut to those areas at this time. Instead, they were brought to Macedonia (v. 10).

It is in Philippi, a leading city of Macedonia, that the disciples, on the Sabbath, go outside the city gate to the river, where they expect to find a place of prayer (vv. 12-13).[1] So they stop, and before doing anything else, they pray.

Or at least, they seek to find a place to pray. Because as they sit down by the river, instead of praying, they meet some

---

1. This location by the river would have been the place where the women could go through the appointed Jewish service of prayer for the Sabbath day (F. F. Bruce, *Acts*, 311). The place of prayer also became the place of proclamation.

of the women who have gathered there. So they proclaim
the gospel to these women and God opens Lydia's heart to
respond to Paul's message (v. 14).[2] Prayer and proclamation
go hand-in-hand because 'the word of the gospel is a word
that comes to a rebel heart. I am a rebel against God. I may
be indifferent to Him, I may be antagonistic to Him, but
I'm actually rebelling against him. He (God) then comes,
by the Bible, and he says, "I am commanding you to do an
about-turn, to repent of your sins and to believe in me."
And the individual says, "There is no way that is going to
happen! It will take a miracle for that to happen!" Yes it
will. That is the miracle of regeneration.'[3] And that is what
we see in Acts 16. Here we see the people of God, knowing
the sovereign oversight of God in His mission, planning to
pray, depending on God, yet ready to proclaim the gospel
when any opportunity arises. And Lydia is born again
into a living hope. Those who are mindful of prayer, are
prepared to proclaim.

Here are the words of Colossians 4:2-6 in action: *devote
yourselves to prayer, being watchful and thankful. And pray
for us too, that God may open a door for our message, so that
we may proclaim the mystery of Christ...; make the most of
every opportunity.* The key words: devote... being watchful
and thankful... God to open a door... we may proclaim...
make the most of every opportunity. It's praying with our
eyes wide open, motivated, ready, and available.

Similarly as we reach Acts 16 we again find the church
leaders under immense persecution. But yet again, instead

2. The same pattern of prayer then proclamation can be seen in the story
of the female slave in Acts 16:16.
3. Alistair Begg, sermon quoted in Shai Linne, 'Regeneration', Track 7,
Lyrical Theology Vol. 1, (Philadelphia; Lampmode Recordings, 2013).

of responding with groaning and cursing, we read in Acts 16:25 of Paul and Silas praying and singing hymns. What sort of men were these? Tertullian said: 'the legs feel nothing in the stocks when the heart is in heaven'.[4] Paul and Silas were Christians who knew their life was hidden with Christ in God (Col. 3:3). Death was not a threat to their future hope. In fact, Paul wrote 'to live is Christ and to die is gain' (Phil. 1:21). Therefore, prayer and hymn singing were perfectly natural actions. It was this gospel mindset that enabled them to be ready for what came next: the earthquake and the prison doors opening. This mindset also enabled them to be ready to speak the gospel into the lives of the Philippian jailer and his whole household, and be part of their dramatic conversion (v. 34).

One implication of Paul's praying is that we might need to broaden our concept of prayer. David Powlison has noticed three emphases of biblical prayer:

1. Sometimes we ask God to *change our circumstances*: heal the sick, give us daily bread, protect us from suffering and evildoers, make our political leaders just, convert our friends and family, make our work and ministries prosper, provide us with a spouse, quiet this dangerous storm, send us rain, give us a child.

2. Sometimes we ask God to *change us*: deepen my faith, teach us to love each other, forgive our sins, make us wise where we tend to be foolish, make us know You better, enable us to sanctify You in our hearts, don't let us dishonour You, give us understanding of Scripture, teach us how to encourage others.

3. Sometimes we ask God to *change everything by revealing Himself* more fully on the stage of real life, magnifying

4. F. F. Bruce, *Acts*, p. 317.

the degree to which His glory and rule are obvious:
Your kingdom come, Your will be done on earth as it is
in heaven, be exalted above the heavens, let Your glory
be over all of the earth, let Your glory fill the earth as
the waters cover the sea, come Lord Jesus.[5]

Paul often moved between these three emphases in
prayer. He engaged God in prayer for help with his
circumstances; he prayed asking for wisdom for living, and
he prayed for the bigger picture of gospel growth through
his circumstances.

How can we grow in this joy and trust in God despite
the circumstances? How can we grow in an awareness of
God, His purposes and plans, His goodness and grace?
A hymn of the Jewish people, that people like Paul would
have grown up singing and memorising, was:

The Lord is my light and my salvation –
whom shall I fear?
The Lord is the stronghold of my life –
of whom shall I be afraid?

When the wicked advance against me
to devour me,
it is my enemies and my foes
who will stumble and fall.

Though an army besiege me,
my heart will not fear;
though war break out against me,
even then I will be confident.

One thing I ask from the Lord,
this only do I seek:
that I may dwell in the house of the Lord

5. David Powlison, 'Pray Beyond the Sick List', p.4.

all the days of my life,
to gaze on the beauty of the Lord
and to seek him in his temple (Psalm 27:1-4).

As Ed Welch says in *When People are Big and God is Small*: 'if you can read [or sing] this psalm and say that it expresses the desire of your heart, then your fear is not a sinful fear of man.'[6] It is a wholehearted trust in God as the sovereign overseer of our lives, our stronghold – in whom we don't have to be afraid. The Apostle Paul developed and deepened this truth when he wrote in Romans 8:31-9:

> *What, then, shall we say in response to these things? If God is for us, who can be against us? He who did not spare his own Son, but gave him up for us all – how will he not also, along with him, graciously give us all things? Who will bring any charge against those whom God has chosen? It is God who justifies. Who then is the one who condemns? No one. Christ Jesus who died – more than that, who was raised to life – is at the right hand of God and is also interceding for us. Who shall separate us from the love of Christ? Shall trouble or hardship or persecution or famine or nakedness or danger or sword? As it is written:*
>
> > *'For your sake we face death all day long;*
> > *we are considered as sheep to be slaughtered.'*
>
> *No, in all these things we are more than conquerors through him who loved us. For I am convinced that neither death nor life, neither angels nor demons, neither the present nor the future, nor any powers, neither height nor depth, nor anything else in all creation, will be able to separate us from the love of God that is in Christ Jesus our Lord.*

Just like Paul in Acts 16, people in prayer are people prepared for anything that comes their way.

6. Edward T. Welch, *When People are Big and God is Small*, (Phillipsburg, New Jersy; P & R, 1997), pp. 60-61.

Final Words

It is impossible to read the Book of Acts and miss the importance of prayer in the life and ministry of the early church. The growth of the church was and will always be powered by the prayerful proclamation of the word of His grace. Acts teaches us that a distinguishing mark of a Christian and of a truly Biblical church is that they pray. Prayer undergirds the life and ministry of the church – being both private and corporate in nature. Prayer in Acts includes prayer for healing, prayer for sending out missionaries, prayer for church leaders, prayer for boldness in proclaiming the gospel to an apathetic or hostile world.

One aspect of prayer though, that the Book of Acts doesn't address, is the guilt that is often attached to prayer. This little book is a re-call to united prayer – the ordinary, everyday praying life of a Christian. But I would hate for this book to leave people with the dominant feeling of guilt for not praying enough. For sure, guilt might be a valid response as prayerlessness is often the mark of sinful, slack or sleepy Christians. But guilt can and should never be the last word. The last word for Christians is always grace. And it is grace which is the motivator and sustainer of our prayers.

In a profoundly paradigm-shifting sermon preached at a conference in Brisbane in January 2013, Gary Millar[1] spoke

---

1. Gary Millar is the Principal of the Queensland Theological College; the conference was the Ignite Training Conference, a ministry of the Queensland Christian Convention Association. Gary has further developed his biblical theology of prayer in *Calling on the Name of the*

of learning to pray in a distracted, fallen world. In fact, according to Millar, God has designed prayer to work in a fallen world. Prayer is an interim measure. It's temporary. We know this because there was no prayer in the Garden of Eden (Gen. 1-2), and in the new heaven and the new earth (Rev. 21-22), there won't be any more prayer, for we will see and speak with God face to face! (1 John 3:2).

Prayer is designed for this world where we feel discouraged and hurt by our sin and the sins of others against us. But before we get despondent, Millar calls us to be encouraged with these three things:

1. God has made prayer possible through the gospel. Without the gospel, prayer simply can't happen. Galatians 4:4 reminds us that because we are God's children, we have the spirit of God which helps us cry out Abba, Father.

2. God made prayer good in a fallen world through the gospel. God says He will show up when we pray. He is always listening, and even when it feels like a distracted prayer time, it's still good, powerful and productive. If you are distracted when praying, that makes sense, because prayer was made for people with wandering minds.

3. God has promised he will answer our prayers in a fallen world through the gospel. Like a child to their parents, we can ask anything and trust God with the answer. And because we can trust God we can ask anything of Him (Phil. 4:6-7).

Lord: A Biblical Theology of Prayer [NSBT: Leicester; Apollos and Downers Grove, Illinois; IVP Academic, 2016)

Reading the Book of Acts provides us with the original call to extraordinary, united prayer. Jonathan Edwards noticed this, and called Christians to pray. Extraordinary united prayer is otherwise known as the ordinary Christian life, and corporately, is known as the ordinary church prayer meeting. Like 200 years ago, Martyn Lloyd-Jones' plea was clear in 1959 and is a rallying cry to us all today:

> How many of us have stirred ourselves up to take hold of God? How many? This is typical Biblical teaching; this was also the teaching of our fathers. They waited upon God and cried and cried until He did rend the heavens and come down. Let us lay hold upon Him and plead with Him to vindicate His own truth and the doctrines which are so dear to our hearts, that the Church may be revived and masses of people may be saved.[2]

Indeed, may our churches be strong in the Word and prayer, and may we see revival in our day as the gospel continues to go forth, as God brings the multitudes of the lost under the Lordship of Christ, as well as matures His church till we see Him in glory.

---

2. Martyn Lloyd-Jones, 'Revival: An Historical and Theological Survey,' 1959, in *The Puritans: Their Origins and Successors* (Edinburgh; The Banner of Truth Trust, 1987), pp. 1-23.

Christian Focus Publications

Our mission statement –

STAYING FAITHFUL

In dependence upon God we seek to impact the world through literature faithful to His infallible Word, the Bible. Our aim is to ensure that the Lord Jesus Christ is presented as the only hope to obtain forgiveness of sin, live a useful life and look forward to heaven with Him.

Our books are published in four imprints:

CHRISTIAN
FOCUS

Popular works including biographies, commentaries, basic doctrine and Christian living.

CHRISTIAN
HERITAGE

Books representing some of the best material from the rich heritage of the church.

MENTOR

Books written at a level suitable for Bible College and seminary students, pastors, and other serious readers. The imprint includes commentaries, doctrinal studies, examination of current issues and church history.

CF4•K

Children's books for quality Bible teaching and for all age groups: Sunday school curriculum, puzzle and activity books; personal and family devotional titles, biographies and inspirational stories – because you are never too young to know Jesus!

Christian Focus Publications Ltd,
Geanies House, Fearn, Ross-shire,
IV20 1TW, Scotland, United Kingdom.
www.christianfocus.com